Ernest Thompson Seton, Ralph Hoffmann, Jenny H. Stickney

Bird World

A Bird Book for Children

Ernest Thompson Seton, Ralph Hoffmann, Jenny H. Stickney

Bird World
A Bird Book for Children

ISBN/EAN: 9783744731959

Printed in Europe, USA, Canada, Australia, Japan

Cover: Foto ©Andreas Hilbeck / pixelio.de

More available books at **www.hansebooks.com**

BIRD WORLD

A BIRD BOOK FOR CHILDREN

BY

J. H. STICKNEY

ASSISTED BY

RALPH HOFFMANN

———•———

BOSTON, U.S.A.

GINN & COMPANY, PUBLISHERS

The Athenæum Press

TO ITS PUBLISHERS AND ESPECIALLY TO

Mr. Justin H. Smith

UNDER WHOSE AUSPICES IT WAS BEGUN

AND TO WHOSE KINDNESS AND COUNSEL I OWE SO MUCH

THIS LITTLE BOOK IS DEDICATED

AS A TOKEN OF GRATITUDE AND REGARD

PREFACE.

IT may be of interest to some of our readers to know under what guidance they are to make this little journey into the borders of Bird World.

First, then, the plan and direction come from the author of some books they have known as the Stickney Readers. It may be thought worth while to venture on this new pleasure trip under the same leadership.

Second, a gentleman has been found to act as special conductor, — one who has lived closer to Bird World than any of us. For years he has known by sight and sound all our New England birds, and many, if not most, of our chance summer and winter visitors, beside having particularly intimate acquaintance with some which we too shall be glad to meet. A number of the stories which follow are based upon his own personal observations. You will find his name upon the title page. He is a director in the Audubon Society for the Protection of Birds, which makes it certain that the citizens of Bird World are as safe in his hands as are we. You have thus the combined powers of two who are both friends of young people and of birds.

A third point of interest lies in having true portraits of birds by the distinguished artist, Mr. Ernest Thompson Seton, for which you must thank our generous publishers, as also for the color photographs which help us to see better how the living birds we are learning to recognize really look. A number of other kindnesses have helped us to make this book attractive and instructive. The use of drawings by Mr. Ridgway was most kindly allowed us by Dr. Merriam, of the Department of Agriculture, at Washington. Other sketches were made for us by Mr. Knobel, and by arrangement with the publishers of the *Osprey* we have the use of several attractive portraits and sketches. For the use of the Snowy Egret we are indebted to Miss S. J. Eddy.

We also express our obligation to visitors we have met in Bird World, some of whose names occur in our record, for bits of testimony and song. In return we commend the books they have given to the world to be read when this "younger book" has prepared you for them. Among them are : *Birds of Village and Field*, Miss Florence Merriam; *Citizen Bird*, Mrs. Mabel Osgood Wright ; *Winter Neighbors*, Neltje Blanchan ; *Bird Life*. F. A. Chapman ; and the writings of Mrs. Olive Thorne Miller.

CONTENTS.

	PAGE
The Goldfinch	1
The Phœbe	3
Verses	6
The Robin	7
The Oriole	11
Heralds of the Summer	13
The Bluebird	15
The Coming of the Birds	18
The Indigo Bird	19
The Story of a Grouse	21
Bird Acquaintance	24
Bills of Fare	26
Gull Dick	29
Verses	30
The Owl	31
The Scarlet Tanager	36
The Politest Bird	37
A Family of Backwoodsmen	40
The Downy Woodpecker	41
The Flicker	44
The Sapsucker	47
A Second Sparrow Study	49
The Song Sparrow and the Chipping Sparrow	51
How Birds Pass the Night	54
The Blue Jay	56
Bird Homes	58
The Nest as an Oven	59

	PAGE
The Kingbird	63
The Warbler Family	67
A Clever Wren	68
Audubon and the House Wren	69
The Wren	70
At the Bath	73
The Catbird	75
Verses	78
Nest Builders	79
The Swallows	84
Verses	85
The Barn Swallow	86
The Red-winged Blackbird	89
About Birds' Toes	91
Bob White	95
Audubon and the Phœbes	98
How Young Birds Get Fed	99
Food of Birds	100
When a Bird Changes his Clothes	103
A Bird in the Hand	106
Bird Passports	113
The Bird of Many Names	117
The Bobolink	119
Gypsy Birds	121
Foster-Mothers	123
Two Father Birds	126
Born in a Boat	128

viii CONTENTS.

PAGE

How the Wood Duck Gets her
   Young to the Water . . . 130
The Great Caravan Route . . 131
Bird World in Winter 135
Bird Lodgings in Winter . . . 138
   Verses 139
The Eagle 140
The Chickadee 141
A Bird-Paradise 142
   Verses 143
The Sea-Gull 144
A Great Traveler 145
The Redstart 150
The Humming Bird 151
As Free as a Bird 155

PAGE

To the Great and General Court
   of Massachusetts 158
Birds' Enemies 162
Families in Bird World . . . 169
Feathers and Flight 172
   Flight 178
The Snowy Egret 180
The Wood Thrush 183
The Brown Thrush 184
Hawks 186
Bird Language 190
Some Strange Bird Music . . . 193
Bird Bills 195
Appendix 199
Index 212

FULL-PAGE ILLUSTRATIONS AND COLORED PICTURES.

PAGE

A Pair of Goldfinches 1
Robin . . . . . colored . 9
Oriole . . . . . " . 12
Yellow Warbler . . " . 13
Bluebird . . . " 16
Owl . . . . . " 33
Scarlet Tanager " 36
Cedar Bird . . . " . 37
Downy Woodpecker . " 40
The Song Sparrow 51
A Pair of Kingbirds 64

PAGE

Louisiana Water Thrushes . . 67
A Happy Pair 84
Part of a Quail Family . . . 96
Black-throated Green Warblers . 100
Winter Life 136
Herring Gulls and their Nesting-
   Places 144
The Redstart 150
A Pair of Orioles 156
A Useful Hawk 188
The Wood Thrush 192

A PAIR OF GOLDFINCHES

BIRD WORLD.

THE GOLDFINCH.

SINCE there must be a first bird for us to meet in this long visit we are to make together in Bird World, and some of us have to choose which one, suppose we let it be the pretty confiding Goldfinch, who with his mate shall stand upon the threshold to receive us.

This old pasture where little grows but weeds and thistles is a favorite place with the Goldfinches. Thistlebird is one of the names by which they are known. There is no merrier bird than the Goldfinch. He spends the pleasantest part of the year, the spring months, when other birds are busiest, singing and enjoying the sunshine. When winter comes, instead of leaving us he stays with a happy company of friends, feeding on weeds that stand above the snow, twittering and calling sweetly to his companions. It is not strange, then, that the Goldfinch has many friends and no enemies.

The little Goldfinches are cradled in the softest of silk — nothing less than thistledown. With this the mother lines the nest, which is generally built late in June, when thistles have begun to ripen. The thistle is a good friend to the Goldfinch, for its seeds are a favorite food.

When the little Goldfinches leave the nest, they are by no means as brightly colored as their father. No canary-colored vest or black cap is provided for them, but very sober brownish suits. When April comes again, you will see some of them looking a little brighter, and in a few weeks they will come into as bright plumage as their father. The others, the females, still keep the darker color, like their mother.

The Goldfinch flies in great curves, and as he goes downward he begins a pretty little twitter which he finishes on the upward curve. Through the wide air, over fields and farms, he swings along with his bright " De-*dee*-de, de-*dee*-de, de-*dee*-de." Not the coldest or wettest weather can make him utter a complaining note. Perhaps you know some boy or girl who is cheerful and lively all the day and all the year.

THE PHŒBE.

NEAR Boston there is a little stream celebrated by an American poet who loved birds. It is called Beaver Brook, and the scenery about it is so beautiful that, partly by gift and partly by purchase, a large tract of land has been set apart for a Park, or Reservation as it is called, so that its beauty can be preserved and people be free to visit it whenever they wish.

Fig. 1. — Phœbe.

At the head of the brook are two ponds, and between the two is a little bridge under which the water all the year rushes foaming and splashing. When the poet Lowell used to visit the brook, there was a mill at this spot, and the foaming water used to turn a big mill wheel and help the dusty miller grind the grain which his neighbors brought.

About the last of March every year a citizen of Massachusetts, who has spent the winter farther south, returns to the spot and calls out his name from the trees about the shore, " Phœ-bee ! Phœ-bee ! " stopping now and then to dart over the water for a gnat or fly, and snapping his tail when he returns to the tree.

An old man who has lived in the neighborhood for many years says that when he was a boy, seventy years ago, the Phœbe came every year just as it does to-day, and he and his sister visited the mill every April to find the neat, well-built nest which the bird placed on the rafters of the mill.

The buzzing and whirring of the wheel, and the grinding sound made by the heavy millstones did not disturb either the parent birds or their young. The miller knew them and gladly let them use his roof for shelter.

The boy and his sister loved them too, and never stole the nest nor frightened them. To-day the mill is torn down, but on the very spot where it stood they find the bridge, and under it the strong beams that support it. Here they still build their nest ; the water foams and splashes below them ; people, and sometimes horses and wagons, tramp over them, but they have no fear. In spite of all the changes, they prefer their old home to any other.

The old man and his sister must soon pass away,

and even the younger people who now visit the spot will sometime die too, but if the state, which now owns the ponds, leaves the bridge and the trees and bushes on its banks, I feel sure that every springtime the Phœbe's note will be heard in the last days of March, and the pretty moss-covered nest will be built under the bridge.

The young birds will learn to fly off and catch insects on the wing, and will snap their tails too, as their parents do ; and some day, when their parents die, they will come and build nests under the bridge. No one knows when they first came to this spot, nor how long they will continue to return.

Note. — It was my happy privilege to live for seven years in the cottage upon the estate to which the ponds belonged before Massachusetts made a present of them to all its nature-loving citizens.

It must have been this same Phœbe who called to me from the pine grove across the street so often in its plaintive way. Once when I was ill I took turns in fancying, first, that Phœbe was lost and wished to be found ; and, second, that some one was staying away too long and must be called home to ease an anxious heart. But the note is hardly like a call ; it sounds more like a sweet, loving memory that takes this way of expressing itself. How glad I should have been then to know that I was living at the ancestral home of this ancient family !

J. H. S.

WHY ROBIN DID NOT SING IN THE SOUTH.

IF I ever tried a note
Something rose within my throat.

'T was because my heart was true
To the north and springtime new ;

My mind's eye a nest could see
In yon old forked apple tree !

EDITH THOMAS.

FIG. 2. — Robin.

THEY'LL come again to the apple tree, —
Robin and all the rest, —
When the orchard branches are fair to see
In the snow of blossoms dressed,
And the prettiest thing in the world will be
The building of the nest.

MRS. M. E. SANGSTER.

THE ROBIN.

LONG before you are awake, the Robins have had a morning meeting, sung a very jolly chorus, visited two or three cherry trees, and by the time you have breakfasted and come out to play, they are taking a second meal on the lawns.

Watch one for a moment and then try to tell how he looks. He is larger than a Sparrow, — nearly twice as large ; his bill is longer, sharper, and is bright orange in color.

Robin's head is wholly black, not patched like that of the Sparrow; his back is brown, and his breast much the color of your Jersey cow.

Instead of squabbling and scratching in the middle of the street, or flying off in flocks to houses or tree-tops, he stands straight and dignified, his plump breast showing clearly against the green grass, or runs a few steps and then draws himself up stiffly again.

Fruit is very dear to the Robin. Cherries in summer, strawberries in spring, and cedar berries in winter. But when you see him on the lawns, he is hunting for food which only a fish would care to share with him. He braces himself on his feet and pulls and pulls, till the poor worm he is seeking has

to let go, and after some hard pounding by Robin's
sharp bill, it is carried off to the nest for the little
ones, or gulped down by Robin himself.

Mr. James Russell Lowell calls the Robin's nest
"an adobe house." Perhaps some of you have read
how people in Colorado build houses of dried clay,
which bakes in the sun. This is called adobe, and
both the Robin and the Swallow know how to build
in this fashion.

Four eggs of "robin's egg blue," laid early in May,
hatch into very ugly and very hungry youngsters.
Their big yellow mouths are opened wide whenever
the mother or father comes near. These parents are
kept busy all day and every day for a fortnight till the
young birds grow big, till feathers cover their naked
little bodies, and one of them steps to the edge of the
mud nest and looks out.

This is an anxious time for the parents. Soon the
boldest youngster tries his wings and makes for a
neighboring twig. If he misses it and flutters down
to the ground, the parents fly back and forth, making
a great outcry which collects many other birds. If
no cat comes prowling about, the little one tries again
and perhaps gets safely off, but often a bunch of gray
feathers tells the sad story of his short life.

When the young birds who escape all the dangers
from cats and hawks, are strong enough to find food

for themselves, the parents build another nest and rear another brood. Meanwhile the first brood fly each night to some neighboring grove where they are joined by other young Robins from miles around. The birds assemble in such numbers that the pattering of their

Robin.

wings on the leaves, while they are arranging their places for the night, sounds like falling rain.

Not only do the young birds come to these " roosts," as they are called, but father-Robins also, who cannot help their wives after sunset, join their children, or perhaps show them the way.

One gentleman, who watched a family of Robins near his house, writes : " The female came and took possession of the nest for the night. I saw her brooding the young till it became so dark that I could distinguish nothing. On the following evening the male fed the young at about the same hour, then flew to the top of a spruce tree, and after singing a good-night to wife and babies, took a direct flight for the roost. The female then fed the young and settled herself in the nest."

By the time you have learned the birds' names, and begun to watch their habits, you may wonder whether there is anything new for you to find out.

You may think, that if so many people have studied them for a hundred years, they will have found out all their interesting ways. But do not be discouraged. Nothing could be more interesting than this habit of the Robins of assembling every summer night in these great companies; and yet, though the Robin is everywhere common, and has been studied by hundreds of bird students, it was only eight years ago that anything was written about " Robin roosts."

THE ORIOLE.

IT is in May when woodlands are green with swelling buds and spreading leaves, and fragrant with the sweet wild flowers, that the brilliant Oriole appears among us.

Very early one morning I heard his clear whistle and hastened to find him. He looked down upon me rather inquiringly, as if he wanted to say, " What do you think of me? " and my heart answered, " I think you are beautiful ! "

He was alone for a few days, busy as a bird could be, trying to select a house lot. He flew from tree to tree, in orchard, garden, and yard. A tall, stately elm seems to please him best, and when the shy little lady he is to make his wife is coaxed to the tallest branch, she demurs, as she knows the peril of building there, and with a decision he does not quite relish she tells him a lower branch would suit her better.

She begins very soon to collect materials for building, singing as she works, making long journeys for the hair and twine necessary for her home. After nest come eggs, and after eggs baby birds. The proud and happy father shows his love as well by the care he takes, and the watchfulness, as by the songs he pours from his full throat. Often he seems to say to the mother, "Run out now and stretch a

Oriole.

little"; and she goes, but not for very long. Why is it that mothers think no one can be quite so content and happy with their babies as themselves?

Summer Warbler, or Yellowbird.

HERALDS OF THE SUMMER.

IF we make a residence in Bird World in such a place
that our doors and windows open out upon hedges
or shrubbery, or upon a garden, we shall not need to
search for this little bird in the picture.   He will come
to us with his pretty yellow mate.

The gentleness of the summer Yellowbirds wins our love. They are as sunny in their temper as in their looks. " Pretty is that pretty does " never need put them to shame.

The Cowbirds have long since found it out and, like the naughty birds they are, have taken advantage of it; but gentle people, if they will not quarrel, will not always suffer their own plans to be turned aside. The Cowbird sometimes finds his match, as we shall see. The following little word-picture will show you how a Yellowbird's nest looked to Mr. Keyser, and what the bird did when she found herself imposed upon.

" The nest of the Summer Warbler was a dainty structure, composed of downy material, and deftly lodged among the twigs of a sapling at the foot of a cliff. A cold spring gurgled from the rocks near by; the willows and buttonwood trees bent to the balmy breeze, and the tinkling of the brook mingled with the songs of many birds.

" Our little strategist comes home and finds a Cowbird's egg dropped into her nest. She begins forthwith to add another story, and this leaves the interloper in the cellar, with a floor between it and her warm breast. I have found several of these exquisite towers that were three stories high, in the top of which the little bird sat perched like a goddess on the summit of Olympia."

DO you believe that a Bluebird would think of coming to New England in February?

One bright, crisp morning in the last month of winter, I heard a clear, lively, little song that I knew, and of course I hastened to find my friend, the Bluebird. The "Blue Robin" little children sometimes call him, and indeed he is a cousin to the Robin family.

He was very cunning at hiding in the old apple tree, and very shy when I found him.

Soon there was a nest, and a little later a family of five, one being a guest who had traveled north for the first time, perhaps, and was not in haste to have the care of a family. He never did any work, but flitted about as if made simply to enjoy himself and be admired.

If you had seen him, you would have thought it very natural. Such a putting together of heavenly blue, and warm, rich, yellowish red would be enough to turn any head that was not full of earnest purpose.

The home was built by the bird mother in the orchard where I could easily watch it, and we became very good friends, these dear Bluebirds and I. They ate the crumbs I gave them, and my joy in them was complete when they came boldly to my door.

Bluebird.

Mother Bluebird, as perhaps you may know, is more quietly dressed than her gallant mate. It is not that she would not take good care of a bright costume, for birds are tidy in their persons; but she thinks more of safety than of looks, and it might be inconvenient to have to fly out of harm's reach just when home could least spare her.

A pair of Robins with very red breasts built a nest close by, and seemed to be good neighbors. How did I know, do you ask? Well, for one thing they formed a chorus, and before sunrise I would hear them singing together.

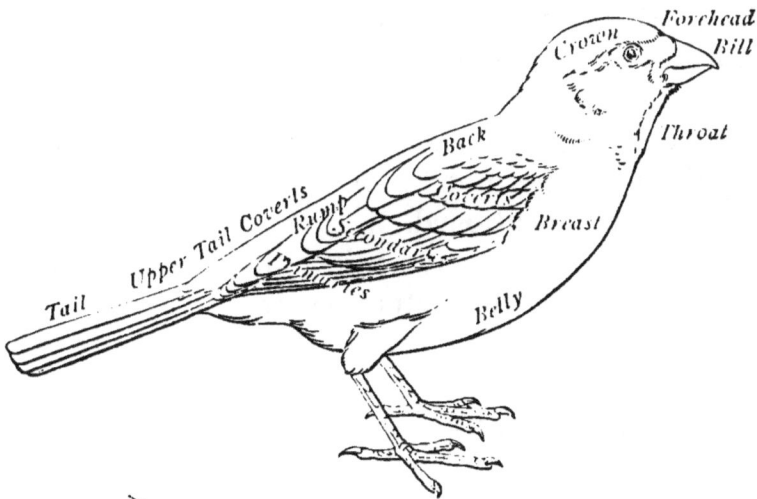

The above diagram explains some names often used in describing a bird.

THE COMING OF THE BIRDS.

IN the lesson on the Oriole you read that he came in May when buds were bursting into flowers. I wonder whether you asked yourself, as you read, where he had come from and why he had not come before.

These are questions that the very wisest men have found it hard to answer. Without hurrying to answer them now, — for if you read further there will be more about these things, — let us ask some country boy when the birds come back and which come first.

If our friend has sharp eyes and ears, he will know that early in March he hears the first Robin, and with him come the gentle Bluebird, the noisy Blackbirds, and the cheery Song Sparrow. The Phœbe waits a fortnight till the flies and gnats begin to stir, for his food does not lie on the ground like that of the birds just mentioned.

In April come many more birds, but May is the great month for the returning tribes. The names alone of all those that come in the warm days of early May would fill a page. Bird World in the north is like a seaside summer place, very empty in winter, but stirring with life in summer.

THE INDIGO BIRD.

NOW that we are on Bluebirds, let us give a thought to a smaller Bluebird without the bright breast.

The Indigo bird seems to be all blue till, looking closely, we see a greenish cast in some lights, and a trace of brownish color on under parts and wings and tail.

The Bluebird, as I told you, though smaller than the Robin, is a near relative ; the Indigo bird is perhaps as near a cousin to the Sparrow. Lady Indigo wears brown for the most part, only adding her husband's "colors," as a good wife should, on shoulders and outer tail webs.

This is a wise precaution, for these birds do not carry on their family affairs high out of harm's way, but build a nest in a low bush or on tall, stiff grasses. They will build by the roadside sooner than close by our homes, and they do not respond with confidence to our friendly advances.

But, while they nest and feed on or near the ground, you will most often see one swinging from a topmost twig of a tall tree, when its song makes you search for the singer.

Do not look for them among the very earliest birds; they make up to us for coming later to the bird concert of the year, by singing away on in August, when many of the other birds are resting their voices. If you are walking or riding on a country road well lined with shrubs and trees, I should be surprised if you do not before summer ends, looking up, see the male Indigo bird — a little blue canary you will think — on the outer end of a high twig; or, once in a summer, you may come upon the dust-colored mother dusting herself as mother-hens do, and coming from her bath feeling as clean as you do coming from yours.

What if the sky is clouded?
What if the rain comes down?
They are all dressed to meet it
In waterproof suits of brown.

BLUEBIRD.

"So the Bluebirds have contracted, have they for a house?
And a nest is under way for little Mr. Wren?
Hush, dear, hush! Be quiet, quiet as a mouse."

THE STORY OF A GROUSE.

I WAS born in the swamp at the foot of this hill, under the laurel; and as soon as I broke through the shell, I ran off over the dry leaves with my brothers and sisters.

There were ten of us, and from June, when we were born, till August we kept close to our mother. The whole family wandered here and there through the swamp, and though we children sometimes ran off too far, we found each other again by peeping and by listening for our mother's cluck.

Once a man and two children came upon us suddenly and we all hurried off among the leaves, where we squatted down and kept as quiet as we could. Our mother, however, ran out in front of the man, trailing her wings close to the ground, and keeping his attention till she felt sure we were well hidden. Then she ran off through the bushes. Presently we heard her cluck and each of us answered with a faint peep and one after another we came out from our hiding places. Then our mother took us quickly off into the deep bushes to a place of safety.

We found enough to eat all summer; berries were plentiful and we became skilful in catching the spiders and beetles that ran over the ground. When we were very little we spent the night under our mother's wings, poking our heads out through the feathers when it grew light.

What we disliked most was the cold rain that sometimes fell, chilling us through our feathers, and preventing us from finding food.

We kept together till the fall and since then, though there are many Grouse in these woods, we have never had a family reunion. By the fall, too, we had all learned to fly pretty well; we were strong of wing, and at night we flew into trees and roosted on the branches.

Now began the season when men came into the woods to shoot us, and though I escaped myself, I often saw the fallen feathers of less fortunate birds.

The sound of the guns, and an experience I had with a fox who almost caught me because I was roosting too near the ground, taught me a valuable lesson, so that now, without boasting, I may claim to be a pretty wary old bird.

I well remember the falling of the first snow in November, and yet I was not so surprised as you might imagine. It seemed natural to see the white masses covering the vines and leaves ; and I found that feathers had grown on my toes so that it was almost as if I walked on snowshoes. When I found out that the buds of many of the bushes were fine eating, I felt no desire to leave the woods where I was born.

So here I stay, year in and year out. In March I have a favorite log where I always drum. You can hear my strokes a mile away, and when I am drumming I spread out my tail and blow out my feathers, till there is no handsomer bird in the swamp.

Each year I see and hear the Ovenbirds that come to rest on my log, and they tell me of their journeys southward in the fall, and the fine woods they find where there is never snow, but I think my own woods are best. I should be a foolish Grouse to fly so far into an unknown country when my feathers keep me so warm and buds are so easy to find.

BIRD ACQUAINTANCE.

HOW many birds are you sure you would know by sight? You can tell an English Sparrow from a Robin or Bluebird, and you would not mistake the Summer Yellowbird or the Oriole perhaps.

Will you not begin to get into closer acquaintance with the citizens of Bird World? Let us stop searching for new birds and study awhile some that we already know. The English Sparrow is the commonest of all, and you will not need to go far to find one.

As I write, there is one within a few feet of me in the pear-tree branches outside my window.

What is it that we wish to know? First, by what marks shall we recognize him when he comes again? The male and female Sparrows differ, and the young at different ages. We will try to remember where this one is slate color, and where brown, where light colored, and where darker, whether the color is in patches, bars, or streaks, whether it shades into another color or ends distinctly. The diagram of a bird on page 17 will help us in stating what we see.

Now we must record what we have learned, to see . if it fits the next Sparrow. This one may be a Cock Sparrow, and that may be a lady-bird; or this may be a bird a year or two old, and the next one but a few months. It will take time to learn them all.

Now we are ready to study the ways of our little visitor in the tree. See him rub his bill, first on this side and then that, against the branch on which he perches. Is it to dry it, or to sharpen it, or to polish it? Half the time it may be only a habit.

He is on a bare branch, but how he pecks and pecks; if you watch, you may see him swallow. When he has gone, go and see if there are grubs or insects in the cracks of the bark.

· While you have been looking, he has hopped to new places to rub his bill and peck as before. He goes to a topmost branch and you see his under parts. The branch is too large for him to grasp with his toes, but he clings, and head and tail help him to keep his balance. Perhaps he will stretch one wing so that its quills stand all apart; and see him lift the little brown feathers under his chin, or where his chin should be. Do you know how much birds can lift and loosen their feathers if they wish, or how tightly they can hug them? If you saw them held loosely on a cold day or night, they would make Cock Sparrow seem a much larger bird.

If you have looked with real interest at one little half-despised Sparrow, something has been left in your heart which will remain and grow.

BILLS OF FARE.

A CERTAIN family in a country town is often joined at dinner by some friends who are content with " just the bones."

Dogs, you will say; but they are not dogs. Turn to page 141 and you will see one of these little guests, and if you look closely you will see that though he cannot get as much off a bone as a dog, yet his beak is stout enough and his eye sharp enough to pick the last bit of gristle.

He does not come to these people's table, but if the window is open he is almost within reach of the children's hands. There is an old apple tree just outside the dining-room, and on its branches there always hangs a ham or mutton bone. This is visited almost every day in winter until it is picked clean.

Sometimes the Downy Woodpecker drills into the tough tendrons, and occasionally a fat bluish gray bird with white under parts — Nuthatch is his name — joins the Chickadees at their feast.

Where are the other winter birds? you will ask. Cannot the little Kinglet and the Creeper have their share?

The people who put out the bones would be glad
enough to welcome them, and from what I know of
the Chickadee's manners, I think he would be the last
to treat them rudely, if they came; but yet they are
never seen clinging to the bone and picking at the
frozen scraps.

To ask a hungry Creeper to have a piece of gristle
would be as cruel as the Stork was to his friend
Reynard. No one is quicker than a Creeper when it
is a question of prying a canker-worm's eggs out of
a crevice in the bark, but he cannot use his slender
bill for such rough work as hacking frozen meat.

Up in Vermont is another family who spread a
table for their bird friends. The bone hung up by
the first family serves the Chickadee for a chair, a
table and food also; but the birds which visit this
family eat a different food, which is spread out for
them on a board nailed to the top of a post. They
have different bills from those of either the bone-
pickers or the Creepers.

. "Finches" do you ask? "Seed eaters?"

Four or five different kinds of Finches come to this
board, Tree Sparrows, Snowbirds, and occasionally
some very pretty rosy-colored birds called Redpoll
Linnets. If you were near enough to the table on
which the food is spread, you could hear the seeds
crack in their strong bills, and though their bills are

so thick they have short points and can pick up very small seeds.

You see you can learn much about a bird's food by examining his bill. You would not need to ask a Sparrow or a Swallow what he would like to eat. But if you made out a bird's bill of fare by his bill alone you might make a very great mistake.

Sometime perhaps you will read about the Toucan, a handsome South American bird whose bill is as thick as his body, and nearly as long. You would expect him to crack Brazil nuts with ease, and would be greatly surprised to see him in the forests of the Amazon chattering with his comrades in the tops of tall fruit trees, and holding in the end of his enormous beak fruit no bigger than a cherry.

Birds' beaks are like tools; some, you can guess at once, are to be used for chiseling or digging; how others are used it is harder to guess; and to understand some we have to find the owner and watch him at his work.

"GULL DICK."

ON the second of October, 1894, the men on a certain lightship in Narragansett Bay were looking eagerly to see whether an old friend had returned to spend the winter with them.

For twenty-two years a Gull had appeared each October and flown about the ship in search of food, till April, when he had disappeared for the summer.

The men on a lightship see so little to amuse them, that they soon noticed this Gull and offered him food. He on his part grew bolder until he learned to visit the ship regularly, as soon as morning came, and to remain near it until it was time for him to return to the rocks, where he spent the night. His favorite food was pork or fish cut into pieces as large as a hen's egg. He came closer to the ship than the other Gulls, and the crew recognized him by certain marks on his wings.

There was much satisfaction aboard the lightship when "Gull Dick" appeared on this particular morning, but he seemed to have taken a long journey, and to have suffered somewhat from storms.

His plumage was ragged and his movements were rather more feeble than they used to be. The men

said to each other, "'Gull Dick' is getting old. This
may be his last winter with us."

They gave him all the food he wanted, for he seemed
very hungry. All through the winter he came regularly for his meals, driving off the other Gulls if they
came too near his food. The crew fed him for the
last time early in April; the next day he doubtless
started for the north, but what happened to him there
no one knows. Old age, or a fierce storm, may have
carried him off, or perhaps another bird attacked
him; at any rate, he failed to return in the fall, and
the men in the lightship have lost their pet, "Gull
Dick."

TO A WATERFOWL.

WHITHER, 'midst falling dew,
While glow the heavens with the last steps of day,
Far through their rosy depths, dost thou pursue
Thy solitary way?

Vainly the fowler's eye
Might mark thy distant flight to do thee wrong,
As, darkly painted on the crimson sky,
Thy figure floats along.

Seek 'st thou the plashy brink
Of weedy lake, or marge of river wide,
Or where the rocking billows rise and sink
On the chafed ocean side?

BRYANT.

THE OWL.

NO one can mistake an owl. In every country where owls are found (and they are found nearly everywhere), their wise-looking, solemn faces are well known. What is it that gives the owl this look, so grave that we have the saying "wise as an owl"?

Look at the picture and notice that the eyes are placed far forward, and that around each large eye is a broad circle or disk of flat feathers. These circles of feathers make the eyes seem even larger, and go far toward giving the bird its solemn look.

An owl's beak and claws are curved and strong. They resemble those of another family which includes the Hawks and Eagles, who also live by violence.

Hawks, if they are robbers, are at any rate like the robber barons of old, dependent on their strength and swiftness as much as on surprise. The owl is more like a stealthy thief, and his success depends almost wholly on silence and secrecy. Twilight is his favorite time, or moonlight nights. His feathers, moreover, are edged with such soft down that an owl might pass directly over your head and you would hardly hear it.

Think of the whistling of a pigeon's wings and you will see how remarkable this silence is. Here is,

then, the secret of the owl's success, — broad, powerful wings on which he relies for stealthy, noiseless
flight ; large eyes, like a cat's, which gather up all
the dim light ; and sharp, strong claws which seize
and tear his victim.   An owl is a cat on wings.

It was long believed that an owl could not see by
day, and that he hunted on the darkest nights.   Probably neither statement is true.   The owl can see as
well, if not better, in the daytime than we can ; but if
there is no light he cannot see at all.   Why does he
hide by day, you will ask, in the barn or belfry, or in
the hollow tree, and only come out at dusk?

If a pickpocket had a certain mark by which every
one knew him the moment he appeared, it would be
easy to avoid him, and he would probably have to get
his living by honest work; the owl is known the moment he is seen, and the fuss the little birds make
when he happens to appear in the daytime would warn
his victims and keep him hungry till he starved.

No one who has seen an owl surrounded by a crowd
of furious birds, scolding and flying excitedly about,
can forget the scene.   It seems as if they were calling
him " rascal," " thief," and " murderer."   Sometimes a
cheerful little Chickadee, looking over an apple tree,
puts its head into a hollow trunk, and instantly his
feathers bristle, and he calls loudly to his friends,
" There's an owl in here, there's an owl in here!"

Owl.

They answer in the greatest excitement, and all the birds round about come to peer in at the villain. You can imagine, therefore, that the owl does a better business, and leads a more peaceful life, if he puts off his tour of the orchard till evening.

But what do owls find in the twilight when the birds are asleep? Have you ever heard a mouse at night running backward and forward in the walls?

Besides the mice who share your house with you, there are many wild mice in the fields, and they are most active at night. In winter, if snow falls in the night, you may find their tracks all about in the morning. Sometimes the track ends abruptly, there are signs of a scuffle, and perhaps a little blood mark may be seen in the white snow. This is where the poor mouse gave a pitiful shriek as the sharp claws of an owl pierced his back.

Under the apple tree, in whose hollow trunk the owl spends the day, you will pick up curious little bunches — pellets they are called — of fur, and on opening one of them you will find the skull and other bones of a mouse or bird. Instead of picking the flesh off the bones as a hawk would, the owl crushes the skull and large bones, and swallows his victim head first; then in his stomach the indigestible portions, the fur, feathers, or bones, are rolled into this curious pellet and cast forth.

The commonest owl near cities is called the Screech Owl; he is not larger than a small chicken, is reddish gray, with two tufts of feathers like ears. His note is a mournful but gentle wailing sound, and is often heard on moonlight nights in the autumn.

One of these owls spent the winter once in the Washington Elm, and many people saw the little tenant of this famous tree sitting at the edge of his home and sending out his mournful "who, hoo, hoo, hoo" over the Cambridge Common.

The larger owls live in the deep woods, and their hooting is loud and often terrifying to those who first hear it. In the frozen north lives the Snowy Owl, whose brownish feathers turn almost white in winter. On the western plains lives a curious member of the family, the Burrowing Owl. His home is a burrow, often the deserted home of some prairie dog.

The owl has long been much abused and attacked for its sinful manner of life. It is only lately that people have discovered how much good most owls do. Many owls have been shot and their stomachs opened, but instead of small birds being the favorite food, the greater part was found to consist of mice and insects, both of which injure the farmer's crops.

We are sorry that the owl occasionally kills a song bird, but if he is really of such help to the farmer, ought we not to protect him, and when we hear his trembling voice in the still moonlight, think of him not so much as a midnight robber as a sort of policeman guarding the farms, gardens, and fields?

Scarlet Tanager.

THE SCARLET TANAGER.

THE male Tanager gives up its scarlet color when nesting time is over, but wears the velvety jet black of his wings. A dull olive green is the color of the female, and of the male when the scarlet is dropped. Its song resembles that of the Robin, but is not so free and clear.

The Cedar Bird

THE POLITEST BIRD.

WE can all tell what would happen if we should throw a piece of bread into the street, under the trees where the Sparrows are chattering. What

a noisy group there would soon be about the bread;
and if some lucky fellow should fly off with a large
crumb, how the others would hurry after, and leave
him no peaceful moment in which to eat it.

Country boys and girls know, too, how very ill-
mannered even motherly old hens will be, and how
undignified they will look if you throw a handful of
grain into their midst.

You will therefore be surprised, I feel sure, at the
story I am going to tell you about the politest bird I
know. No princess in a fairy tale could be brought
up by her anxious parents to have better manners
than this handsome bird.

His name and his picture you will find on the
preceding page, and some of you who live among the
hills where the red cedars stand covered all winter
with spicy smelling berries, will know from his name
what he eats in winter and early spring.

When you hear that he is called Cherry Bird as
well, you will all know what he eats in summer, and I
think you will wish you could get your cherries as
easily as he can his.

One morning in August a gentleman saw several
Cedar Birds fly into a small tree on which bunches of
wild cherries were hanging. On one limb he saw
two birds sitting side by side, one of them with a
cherry in his beak.

Did he gobble it down as fast as he could, or did the second bird rush at him and snatch it from him?

You will hardly guess what happened. The bird who had the cherry hopped along the limb with a motion which would almost do for a bow, and offered the cherry to the second bird. This one's manners, however, were just as good, and he, too, hopped back and returned the cherry to the first bird.

The cherry was passed in this way from one to the other nearly half a dozen times, each bird making a hop and a bow, as if to say, " I cannot think of eating it; I would much rather that you took it."

We must not expect to find such great politeness as these Cedar Birds showed common among birds; in fact, their food is often so hard to obtain that we cannot blame a hungry bird who has little ones to feed for snatching it as quickly as he can.

If there are no tables set for the birds, where each can find his food at his own place, and no one to set them an example, we shall hardly expect them to have good table manners. We can remember the Cedar Birds, however, and when next we see the noisy Sparrows we will beg them to take a lesson from their politer relatives.

Downy Woodpecker.

A FAMILY OF BACKWOODSMEN.

IN the great forests of Maine and northern New York none of the sounds can be heard which are so familiar to us who live in busy towns — no factory whistles, no bells, no trains of cars with their noisy engines. The stillness is broken only by the distant ring of the wood-chopper's axe.

If you follow the sound, you may come upon a strong, broad-shouldered man, swinging a bright axe and covering the ground around the foot of a tree with the clean, sweet-smelling chips. A little distance off is another wood-chopper, giving such blows that you may sometimes hear him half a mile away. He also strews chips far and wide.

The tool of this second woodman is more like a chisel, and he never parts with it, for it is his long, powerful bill. His neck is tremendously strong, so that by drawing back his head he can strike a blow which tears off great sheets of decaying bark, or even large chips of sound wood.

This wood-chopper, or woodpecker, as he is commonly called, is the largest of his family, and is only found where there are tall trees and plenty of them. Like the lumbermen, he is found only in the wild, unsettled parts of the country, and when the forests are cut down he moves on to fresh woods.

THE DOWNY WOODPECKER.

There are plenty of trees, as you know, among farms or even in the city parks, though they do not form dense forests. Here the smaller members of the

Woodpecker Family, one of whom you may see in the colored picture, find wood enough to keep them well employed.

They visit the orchards and the groves, rapping and chiseling the dead or dying limbs. But why are they so busy, these hewers of wood? With what purpose do they cut into the trees or tear off the bark? If you see one cutting in spring, and watch closely, you will find it working day after day at the same limb, and cutting into it a round hole, which finally becomes so deep that the bird disappears inside, coming out now and then with chips, or flying for food and rest.

This hole is a nest. When it is deep enough, the mother lays five or six pure white eggs, not on straw or hair, but on fine chips which have fallen to the bottom. Here the young are hatched and fed. In a day or two they find the chips a rather hard seat, and climb by their feet to the sides of the hole, till they are ready to peep out into the world outside.

Sometimes in the autumn you will see a woodpecker again drilling a hole, this time for his winter retreat; for the most of these birds spend the winter where they were born. Now, however, the birds work alone, for they have lived in the lonely woods so much that they do not care for company, and each bird keeps pretty much by himself in the daytime, and sleeps in his own home by night.

The woodpecker builds his house with his bill,
just as Abraham Lincoln's father cut the logs for
his house with his sharp axe. Besides this very
important work, the woodpecker's bill is used in
a way that is even more necessary. By its help he
finds food for himself, his wife, and his children.

When we hear him tapping at the dead limb, he is
searching for insects, grubs, and beetles, that live in
the decayed wood; he bores into the wood till he
reaches them, but then his bill cannot open wide
enough in the small hole to seize the grub. What
shall he do? He has not gone as far as this to lose
his prize.

His tongue is as well suited for seizing the insect
as his bill was for finding it. It is
like a whaler's harpoon, and though
he keeps it in his bill he can dart it
out to twice the length of the bill;
and not only is it barbed to seize the grub, but it is
coated with slime so that any little flies or eggs will
be sure to stick to it. Thus, when he has found his
dinner he darts out his tongue, strikes it into the
unlucky grub, and the next moment has despatched
that, and thrust it out for another.

FIG. 3.
Tongue of Woodpecker.

THE FLICKER.

The commonest woodpecker is in several ways so different from the rest of his family that he deserves special mention. He has a number of names, but perhaps is most commonly called the Flicker, from his note, and the Golden-winged Woodpecker, from the golden yellow of the under side of his wings.

FIG. 4. — Flicker.

He is a gay bird if you see him near. He has a red band on his neck, black mustaches, and round, black dots over his gray breast. He lives more commonly among farms than in the deep woods, and in battle he would be no match for his cousins of the backwoods.

Nor could the Flicker chop into the trees at such a rate as they, for his bill is more slender, slightly curved, and not so square at the tip. In fact, to get his favorite food he has no chopping to do. When he finds an ant-hill, he stands on the ground and, darting out his tongue, with accurate aim glues one after another of the helpless victims to its tip.

The little Downy Woodpecker is rarely or never seen on the ground, but the Flicker spends much of his time there. He sits differently, too, when he is on a tree; not along it, like his relatives, but across, as most birds do. If you were to consult the head of the family, the big, black woodpecker of the north, he might shake his head and say, " I am afraid Cousin Flicker is degenerating. If he does not look out and mend his ways, he won't be a woodpecker at all before long."

But how is little Downy able to stand as you see him in the picture, and how does he manage to dodge around the trunk of a tree, as I have often seen him do?

In the first place, his tail feathers are very stiff, and end in such sharp points that by pressing them close to the rough bark he can get a great deal of support from them. You will hear later of another bird, who uses his tail to climb chimneys with. Then, too, his claws are arranged, not like a sparrow's, three in front and one behind, but in pairs, two in front and two behind.

One of the hind pair, however, can be moved off to the side, and with this, if he is suddenly pursued, he can pull himself so quickly to the other side of the tree that even a hawk cannot strike him.

There are many other interesting things to learn

about this Woodpecker Family. The Flickers, for instance, bring up their babies on a strange diet and feed them in a remarkable way. First, they eat the food themselves and prepare it in the stomach for the tender stomachs of the little ones. Then, when they see the wide-yawning beaks of their little nestlings, they put their own far down inside them and pump up the soft food from their own stomachs to give it to their little ones.

None of the woodpeckers, as I have said before, are sociable birds. They do not feed in flocks, though the Flickers do get together a little, and the little Downy is often found in winter with a company of Chickadees, or other small winter birds.

Many of the larger woodpeckers are downright savages, preferring the wild forests, keeping far from men, and when caught, giving fierce blows with their powerful bills, and refusing to be tamed.

A famous lover of American birds, Alexander Wilson, caught a southern woodpecker once, called, from his pure white bill, the Ivory-billed. He took it home, and as he went through the streets, the constant cries of the bird made people stop and stare at him. He left it in his room, but when he returned, after an hour, the brave bird had nearly cut a hole through the window-sash, and would in a few minutes have escaped from his prison. Wilson then tied the bird to his table and went out again, only to find, on his return, that the table was ruined by the powerful blows of the bill. The bird refused to eat and at last died, brave and fierce to the end.

THE SAPSUCKER, OR YELLOW-BELLIED WOODPECKER.

This is the only one of the family that can justly be called the enemy of the farmer, and examination has proved that he does, on the whole, more good than harm.

Figure 5 shows the little pits he drills, in regular lines, in the bark of forest trees and sometimes in apple trees; and when the pits fill with sap he drinks it as if it were nectar itself.

FIG. 5. — Yellow-bellied Woodpecker.

Harmful insects are attracted by

this sap, when it runs, and the number that are destroyed by the birds is thought to balance the loss to the tree, though it sometimes happens that the tree dies in a year or two from being so bled by them.

Those of you who have seen maple sugar made from the sap of the sugar maple will think the bird very cunning to find a sugar camp for his own.

Another woodpecker does an equally curious thing. I was riding one day in a park in southern California, and a tree was pointed out to me that had holes as close as these of the Sapsucker filled with acorns. A woodpecker had bored the holes and filled them for a winter store. The nuts were wedged in so tightly it would not have been easy to get them out. In the same line, but showing even greater intelligence, is the use in Mexico of a hollow stalk. The birds make holes and press acorns through them in autumn, so that they drop one by one till the hollow tube is filled. When other food fails the woodpecker draws out his acorns, not from the place at which he put them in but from the floor of his storehouse.

A SECOND SPARROW STUDY.

THIS time it is a little company of sparrows on the ground. Here we have all the ages and varieties. We call them brown birds; but see the gray, slate, tan, and other browns almost to black.

Trace the colors in wing and tail feathers; note the shapes and sizes of patches. Did you know that the wing feathers were bird finger nails numbered in different species according to their need? Pairs of tail feathers, too, have their convenient length, different in sparrows, swallows, and other species. Watch the sparrows as they rise into the air; some birds which fly well could not do it so easily. The tail helps to tell the story of rising and falling.

Get the wing of a fowl and see from what bones the quills grow out — primary, secondary, and coverts; that is, quills of the hand, quills of the middle joint, and quills of the upper joint.

The cut of the wings and tail would make a bird-study all by itself; we can begin it while we are learning to know the birds.

The size of the bird is another point for study; we begin it when two or more birds are compared.

By this time you have gained more than you can

tell in acquaintance and friendship with the Sparrow, and have help in getting a better look at other birds that have to make their photographs on your eye-cameras more quickly. Who knows that you may not have begun to be a naturalist like Wilson and Audubon in older times, or many men and women now?

When you have a picture in your mind of what all sparrows do, you will add each season odd things that you may see but once, and that perhaps no one has seen but yourself.

It is the fashion to find fault with our English Sparrows; first, for coming to America at all, and then for thriving so. But the first ones did not come of their own accord, and it is not their fault that our air made their voices more sharp than we like. It may be true that they have driven away the song birds we love so well; but even that, they may not have meant to do. One who should know as well as anybody has lately told us that the birds are beginning to understand English Sparrow ways, and soon we may have them all back again. I know one person who would miss the active, cheerful little brownies who stay when other birds are gone.

THE SONG SPARROW.

THE SONG SPARROW AND THE CHIPPING SPARROW.

SOME birds are like the shyest wild flowers, living far from people's homes and very hard to find. Others are like the buttercups and dandelions, which grow everywhere on our lawns and in city parks. I suppose by many people the jolly little dandelions are called weeds. One bird is almost like a weed.

Though he, too, lives along the waysides and in the parks and gardens, no one would compare the Song Sparrow to a weed, for he gives much pleasure by singing a clear, merry song as soon as the February snows have melted. All summer he sings, and on into the fall. Even in the winter, on warm days, he sometimes shows that he remembers his little summer melody.

Look at our beautiful representative opposite, as he rests on the big dock weed over the water and pours out his song. Would you know that he was a sparrow if you had no one to help you?

In the first place, he is about the size of an English Sparrow, though more slender, and his colors are a plain gray-brown. But you have learned that a female English Sparrow is also gray and brown. That is true; many sparrows have these colors, but the gray and brown of the Song Sparrow is in streaks or lines, not in unbroken patches, as in the English Sparrow.

The slender figure, the long tail, and a general neat look will help you to tell the American bird from the foreigner. The Song Sparrow is shy, and will hide in the nearest bush, while you all know we can hardly call the English Sparrow shy.

CHIPPING SPARROW.

Another native sparrow is the Chipping Sparrow. He is still slimmer than the Song Sparrow, and wears a cap of dull reddish brown.

The Song Sparrow builds on the ground, often hiding her nest under a tuft of grass or in a thicket. Chippy builds in bushes and always lines her nest with hairs from a horse's mane or tail. You do not see where the bird gets them? She hunts along the fence or posts, where a horse stands, and finds them caught on some crack in the wood.

You learned when you read about the English Sparrow that the male and female differed in looks, but the male Song Sparrows and Chipping Sparrows look just like the female. It is only when the male flies to the top of a bush or to the limb of a tree, and raising his head pours out a song from his little throat, that you know which is which. Both these birds are much the color of dry leaves, grass, and the ground on which they spend their lives. Can you tell why?

The Chipping Sparrow's name refers to his song, which sounds like the syllable chip repeated quickly, — chip, chip, chip, etc.

These two native sparrows have short, thick bills like that of the English Sparrow, but I think they make better use of them than he does. If you could examine the bill very closely, you would see that, though it is so short and thick, the tip is quite sharp and delicate. With this tip the sparrow picks up seeds so fine that you could hardly see them. Remember that their eyes are not only sharp, but are not so far from the ground as yours. These seeds are then crushed in their strong bills, the husk rolled out and the kernel eaten. All over the ground the little sparrows hunt, and many a weed which would. grow up to plague the farmer is destroyed by them. Hundreds of insects, too, — moths, beetles, and grubs, — they find and eat.

Let us record in our notebooks what we have learned by comparing the three sparrows we have met, — the English Sparrow, the Song Sparrow, and the Chipping Sparrow.

HOW BIRDS PASS THE NIGHT.

YOU must get up very early if you expect to find the birds still asleep; they go to bed as soon as it is dark, and have had their first breakfast long before you are awake.

No one need call them; the first faint light in the east finds them up, ready for a long and active day.

If you should happen to go out before the birds are awake, or should startle them in the evening after they have gone to bed, where do you think you would find them, and how would their beds look?

Many of you, I have no doubt, think of them as sleeping all night in their nests, cuddling close to each other, and warmed and protected by their mother. It is true that for two or three weeks of their lives young nestlings sleep in the nests or holes where they have been hatched, and chicks which have no nests hide their downy bodies under their mother's wings; but this lasts but a short time, and after the young birds leave the nests, at the age of two or three weeks, they never again sleep in a bed.

No stretching out of tired limbs on comfortable mattresses, no soft pillows for tired heads, no tucking in, and no one to say " Good night." All these com-

forts you look forward to when bedtime comes, but
how would you feel to hear your mother say instead,
" It is bedtime now, stand on one leg and go to
sleep "; or if she expected you to hang all night from
a crack in the wall; or, worst of all, if your bed con-
sisted of a pool of water, on which you were peacefully to float with your head tucked under your arm?

Almost all the singing birds, after they leave the
nest, perch on a twig as your canary does, the hind
toe bent around to meet the front toes, the feathers
fluffed out, the head snugly hidden under the wing.

Parrots hang themselves up at night by their beaks,
and woodpeckers in their holes and Chimney Swifts in
chimneys hold themselves up by their feet and their
stiff tail feathers.   Hawks and owls stand upright
while they sleep, but hens and turkeys bend their feet
so that their breasts rest on the perch.   The wading
birds, herons, storks, and also the geese draw up one
foot, hide it in the soft feathers, and close their eyes.

Their balance must be easier to keep than ours.
There are many things besides standing on one foot,
which are easier for birds than for us, and positions
which they take easily when awake naturally suit
them best for sleeping.   If you or I could float as
easily as a duck, and if we wore waterproof down
quilts, a night on an icy lake might seem as pleasant
to us as one in a bed.

THE BLUE JAY.

NO bird can be so noisy when he tries, or so silent when he thinks best, as the Jay. If he is stealing, or thinks he may be suspected of any wrong, he slips off through the branches so quietly that, unless you catch sight of the splendid blue and white of his dress you will hardly know what he is.

FIG. 6. — Blue Jay.

But if he is with two or three jolly friends, and the weather is pleasant, he fills the woods with his screams and calls. They are not sweet sounds, but are not unpleasant to hear, particularly in winter, when few birds are here. Some are like a hawk's cry, and some like an ungreased wheelbarrow.

While the Jay is making these sounds, he often hops up the tree, from one branch to the next, or accompanies his cries with an odd motion of his wings and tail. He is a good deal of a clown, and

as a pet amusing.. He learns to speak a few words,
which is a great thing in a bird.

It is not safe to leave valuables about where he can
reach them, for he is a great collector. When he is
free, he gathers acorns and chestnuts and stores them
in hollow trees.

The Jay has without doubt planted many trees
where they would not otherwise have been found, for
he drops the nuts as he flies off with them, and if
they fall into good soil the Jay's children's children
long after may gather fruit from the trees that will
spring up.

The Jay's neighbors do not like him particularly,
for he has one very bad habit. He cannot resist egg
hunting. But for this he might not be regarded with
disfavor, for he sometimes renders good service. In
fact, when an owl comes into the woods the Jay is
often the first to discover him and announce his
presence to the other birds.

The Jay is closely related to the Crow in this country, and in Europe to the jackdaw and magpie. The
whole family are talkative, bustling birds, very light-
fingered we should call them if they had fingers, but
for all that they are amusing, and we should miss
them if they were gone.

BIRD HOMES.

WE pity any boy who has no home; kind people give money to provide a place where he can have a bed at night, a roof over his head, fire and food. ·

Animals rarely have homes, and yet no one pities them. They have their hair, fur, or shell covering to keep off rain; they sleep on the ground without catching cold, so that they really have no need of a home such as we are accustomed to.

Certain animals, as you probably are already think-- ing, do have caves, dens, or burrows in which they spend the night, the cold or wet weather, or to which they flee for safety. Most of these animals, you will see, are intelligent; in fact, the more wisdom the animal has learned in Nature's great school, the more likely he is to have a place which is his own.

Birds, you will say, are intelligent, and yet they spend the night or rainy weather in thick trees and have no homes.

This is true of most of them, during most of their lives, and from what you know of feathers, you can yourselves tell why they do not need roofs or warmth. But imagine a bird without feathers. He would need warmth and shelter surely. Then think when it is that a bird lacks feathers. In the moulting season? Hardly; few fall at a time, so that he is never wholly without covering. When the bird leaves the shell? That is the time, surely, when he needs protection, and the wise and loving bird-mother goes to work, long before even her eggs are laid, to build the home for her young. This we call a nest; it is really a nursery, is it not, a home, not for the parents, but for the young birds?

THE NEST AS AN OVEN.

The nest is first used as an oven. What does the bird bake in this oven? Where does she get the heat? The last question is the easier and you can answer it yourself by holding your pussy cat against your cheek. Where does the warmth come from? Not all from the fur, but from the warm blood running through her veins.

So the bird's little body is warm, warmer even than your cat's. To keep the warmth of the fire an oven is made with walls and a door; so a nest is often built with walls; the mother herself is the door. When she snuggles down on the eggs very little warmth can escape.

But what is she baking? The eggs themselves. As the little seeds grow or develop when the earth is warm, so the little bodies of the birds grow or develop in the warm eggs, till what looked like nothing but yellow and white liquid hatches out a little bird with claws, beak, and the beginnings of feathers.

All this the bird feels, even if she does not think it as we think thoughts, so that when she is mated and her mate and she have chosen the best spot for their nest, she works very busily at building, or weaving, or

FIG. 7. — Bird Homes.

carpentering, whatever her nature tells her she can do best, and before the eggs are ready she has a nest in which to lay them. (The double nest in the picture is quite a curiosity. It belonged to Chipping Sparrows.)

I have spoken as if all birds felt alike and built nests which all served as ovens and as homes for the young. No one, till he reads or learns a great deal about birds, can imagine what an extraordinary variety of nests there are.

In the first place, a large number of the water birds, ducks, and divers, and all the family to which our hen belongs, do not need a nest in which the young shall stay. For their young come out of the shell warmly clothed in such thick down, that they can either paddle right off in the cool water or run about on the land; we call them chicks, and the others, who are naked and helpless when hatched, we call nestlings. At night their mother's feathers are their beds; no need of a nursery for them.

The eggs have to be baked, however, so that often the nests of such birds are warm and snug, especially if they are in damp or cold places. If the eggs are laid in sunny places, on the hot sea sand or rocks, for instance, there is no need of walls, and in such places the nest hardly deserves the name; it is really nothing but a hollow in the sand or a shelf on the rocks.

Many gulls lay their eggs in this careless way. There are certain cunning animals who like raw eggs very much, and they come prowling about, break the shells, and later eat young birds as well.

Certain birds, to escape these four-legged thieves, have moved up a story and built platforms in the trees. These had to be pretty strong, however, for the mother bird may be large, as in the case of the heron, so that the platform must hold her as well as the eggs. Here is real building to be done; sticks to be laid in a more or less clever fashion. In a later lesson we shall see more of the ways of bird builders.

FIG. 8. — *a*, Egg of Canada Jay; *b*, of Crow Blackbird; *c*, of Woodpecker.

THE KINGBIRD.

IN Wilson's time, Tyrant Flycatcher was the name by which this bird was commonly known, and this name, though clumsier, really tells more about his nature than Kingbird.

A tyrant in Greece was a man who drove out the reigning king or rightful ruler. The eagle has long been called the King of Birds, though by this nothing more was meant than that he was among the most powerful and majestic birds. Even the eagle, however, is attacked and driven off by this Tyrant Flycatcher.

FIG. 9. — Kingbird.

Eagles are scarce to-day, and a battle between the two birds is a rare sight, but it is a common sight to see the Kingbird attack and drive off a Crow — a bird nearly three times as large as himself.

Those of you that have read or heard about the

Spanish Armada remember how the little English ships outsailed the large, unwieldy Spanish vessels, ran close under their guns, fired, and were off again before the Spanish ships could return the fire ; so the Kingbird, mounting above the Crow, darts upon him from above and flies off before the clumsy Crow can strike him.

Occasionally the Kingbird actually settles upon the Crow's head or back, and rides some distance before the Crow can shake him off. When you learn that the Kingbird attacks all birds, great and small, who come near him, and with a harsh twitter drives them away, you will fancy him a very unpleasant bird to have about. But you will have a greater respect for him when you learn that it is only in the breeding season that the Kingbird loses his temper so easily, and it is but fair to say that it is only birds that wander into the neighborhood of his wife and nest that he drives away so rudely.

Flycatcher was the name by which he was known, for outside the swallows we have no more skilful fly-catcher. From the wire on which he is sitting, the post, or the mullein stalk, he flies out a short distance, makes a sweep, and returns to his perch. If you are near him, you hear at some time during his short journey a sharp click, like the snapping of a watch case. That sound means death to some winged insect. All

A PAIR OF KINGBIRDS.

day long the Kingbird sits in some place where he can watch in the air about him, and all day long his bill closes over flies, gnats, and beetles.

Many, if not most, of the insects which he seizes are at some time of their lives harmful to the farmer, so that the Kingbird's work in feeding himself and his children destroys thousands of the farmer's enemies.

A Kingbird's nest is very easily found. You can imagine that a bird that guards his home so thoroughly will take no great pains to conceal it. It is a rather bulky nest, often placed in apple trees, and looks very warm and comfortable. The outside is very apt to be ornamented with clusters of withered flowers of certain plants, and often long strings of pack thread hang from the nest. Inside, the eggs and the young rest on horsehair.

The Kingbird's colors are brown and white, with a dark, almost black, head and tail. Curiously enough, a few feathers on the head are colored bright scarlet, but so few are the feathers and so well concealed, as a rule, that you would see many Kingbirds very near you without ever seeing this red patch.

When the bird is angry, however, or excited, he can, like most fly-catchers, lift slightly the feathers of his head, so that probably many of the birds he has chased have seen more of the red than you have.

The female Kingbird lacks these red feathers, but,

unlike the female Bluebird and Oriole, looks otherwise exactly like the male. See whether this was true of the other fly-catchers of which you have read.

When the Kingbird's young have left the nest, and no longer need protection, the family stay in the north a very short time. By September they have left New England, and in the winter are in Central America. Who of you know why they should leave a country where there are winter frosts? Is it because they themselves are afraid of cold?

I think you would all have liked for once to see the Kingbird get the worst of a battle, which Wilson long ago observed. We all like to see any one who is a little inclined to bully others given a lesson. This Kingbird attacked a Red-headed Woodpecker on a fence rail. Every time he swept down expecting to give the woodpecker a smart rap on the head, the woodpecker pulled with his third toe and slipped around the rail, so that the Kingbird struck only the empty air. The woodpecker saved himself in this way so many times that it seemed to Mr. Wilson that he was enjoying the game. It would not be strange, from what we know of the woodpecker, if he enjoyed a joke. We hardly expect the Kingbird to do so. All kinds of birds have their place, and we honor this one because he is brave and useful.

LOUISIANA WATER THRUSHES.

THE WARBLERS.

YOU have already heard about the Owls and the
Woodpeckers, two families, the members of
which are easy to recognize. The Warblers are
another large Bird World family. They are not
named, as you might well suppose, from their fine
voices, for few of them can sing as well even as your
old friend the Robin. But, like many birds who lack
fine voices, the Warblers make up for their loss by
fine feathers and a very dainty appearance. Yellow,
orange, and blue are very common colors among
them, and they are nearly all small, neat-looking
birds. The Ovenbird, which gets its name from its
oven-shaped nest, is a Warbler, and its cousins, the
Water Thrushes, which you see on the opposite page,
belong, of course, to the same family. You will find
the pictures of three other Warblers in this book :
two of them are the Redstart and the Summer Yellowbird. Can you find the third?

A CLEVER WREN.

WHEN a pair of House Wrens decide that they want to build their nest in a certain place, it takes a good deal to prevent them from doing so. Sometimes several birds, who build in similar situations, all want one particular spot,—a knot hole in a tree or a bird box. Bluebirds, White-bellied Swallows, and House Wrens often struggle violently in nesting time, and, as in other struggles, it is not always the largest bird that wins.

A gentleman once saw a pair of wrens outwit some swallows in the following manner. There had been a long struggle over a box, built on the house, with the usual round hole for an entrance. The wrens had pulled twigs into the box. The swallows had promptly pulled them out. The scolding of the wrens and the sharp twitter of the swallows were heard all day about the box.

One morning the wren was seen hauling along an unusually stout twig, as thick as a lead pencil. It was too heavy to carry straight to the box, but he managed to get it into the lower branches of a pear tree, and finally up to the box. Here he was met by the she-bird, and together they pulled one end into

the hole, and there they fastened it, so that it blocked
the entrance. When the swallows returned, they
could not squeeze past it. They tried to pull it out,
but it had evidently been secured inside. The little
wrens could push past easily; and having now the
field to themselves, raised their brood in peace.

All day long the wren mother goes backwards and
forwards bringing flies and insects or whatever food
she can find. A lover of birds once watched this
bird, and saw her go 278 times in a day.

A number of wrens' nests are unused. One
wonders whether they are built to take refuge in
during severe weather.

AUDUBON AND THE HOUSE WREN.

A Wren lived just outside Audubon's window, and
amused him with his bright song. " Having procured
some flies and spiders," says Audubon, " I now and
then threw some of them towards him, when he would
seize them with great alacrity, eat some himself, and
carry the rest to his mate. In this manner he became
daily more acquainted with us, entered the room, and
once or twice sang while there. One morning, suddenly closing the window, I easily caught him and
held him in my hand, and finished his likeness, after
which I restored him to liberty."

THE WREN.

YOU have all laughed af the old woman who lived in a shoe ; but to a House Wren this would not seem so strange a home. Let me tell you a few of the odd nesting places this bird has chosen.

Generally she builds in a hole in a tree or in a bird box, but almost anything which is hollow inside seems to do. One nest that I saw was in the broken end of a waterspout. Instead of water coming out of it, the little wrens slipped in and out, carrying sticks and straws for a nest.

Another bird thought the inside of an awning would make a fine home, but when the middle of the day came, the awning had to come down to shade the windows, and all the rubbish rolled out. The next morning the bird was up early, and before noon had collected another mass of sticks. Day after day the wren kept up the attempt, declining to make use of a box which was nailed up near by.

Perhaps the strangest story comes from Washington. A workman hung his coat up for a little while, and when he took it down and put his hand in the pocket, he was astonished to find sticks and feathers in it, and even more so when a wren appeared near

by and scolded him
furiously for presum-
ing to wear his own
coat.

He was a kind-
hearted man and would
gladly have lent the
wren his coat pocket
if he had been able to
do' without it; how-
ever, it came out all
right, for he hung up
an old coat instead,
and the happy birds
laid their eggs and
hatched them in the
place of their own
choosing.

House Wrens and
cats are great enemies.
The moment the little
bird spies the cat
prowling about, she

FIG. 10. — Long-billed Marsh Wren.

chatters and scolds, so that all the neighboring birds
know what the trouble is about. I am afraid Pussy
has given the wren good cause now and then to fear
and dislike her.

Our wren is a cousin of Jenny Wren, the favorite of all English children. Jenny is a smaller bird, and she stays in England all the year, while our wren leaves us in the fall for the south, where she can find the insects which she eats.

Like the swallow and the Bluebird, the wren seems glad to make his home near the homes of people, and no one has ever accused him of doing anything but good to the farmer or gardener.

To find the birds of the picture, — the Long-billed Marsh Wrens, — we must go to some soft, wet place, which in early spring may require the use of high rubber boots. These birds are near cousins of the House Wren, but choose to live among the cat-tails. They have learned to weave, and instead of nesting in holes or boxes they make their homes of rushes. Regular basket-work it is, and the almost globular nests hung in the reeds may hold eight or nine chocolate eggs.

HAVE you ever watched a canary going through its morning bath? The thoroughness of the cleansing is only matched by the bird's enjoyment of it. But there is as much more pleasure in seeing a free bird go through its daily wetting and drying and preening as there is in every other free act of a free bird.

Our little street gamins, English Sparrows, choosing a mud puddle rather than go a little out of town for a clean pool, are not worthy to represent the birds of dainty ways.

One of my pleasant bird memories is of a little stream, hardly more than a handbreadth wide, flowing down a hill slope, from a spring in the neighborhood of Saratoga, and making a little nest in the hollow of a rock. I could almost have enclosed the brooklet with my arms and measured its depth with my lead pencil; but for pretty sentiment, and the pleasure it gave to the comers and goers at Elim, the summer cottage of my friend, it will "go on forever." I could fancy the birds saw from afar that single bright spot on the steep hill — a jewel, dropped by a princess of another world, with a ribbon on either side.

The birds did not come to it as early in the morning as I should have expected ; perhaps they liked to
wait till the water should be warmed a little, or perhaps in Bird World a bath after eating is not thought
to be unhealthy. However that may be, from eight
o'clock, in rapid turn, in ones, twos, seldom more than
threes, they kept the little " Bath " in constant use till
evening twilight.

Such water lovers some of them were ! They made
it a shower bath by sending the splashes high over
their heads. They shook each feather in the water
for wetness and out of it for dryness. So clear was
the pure spring water, that it seemed like bathing in
a mirror.

Some of the birds would stop and preen their feathers before they left the spot, but others would go to
the trees to complete their dainty toilets. Boys and
girls who think it a burden to keep their hair in
proper fashion should take a lesson from the birds.
Feathers have their price in care-taking as well as
other beautiful apparel.

It is not probably true that birds are afraid of cold
water. Tree Sparrows will spend from three to five
minutes, it is said, in water that flows directly from
melting snow, acting all the while as if the fluttering
of their wings and tails was perfect glee.

THE CATBIRD.

He sits on a branch of yon blossoming tree,
 This mad-cap cousin of Robin and Thrush,
And sings without ceasing the whole morning long ;
 Now wild, now tender, the wayward song
That flows from his soft, gray, fluttering throat ;
 But often he stops in his sweetest note,
And shaking a flower from the blossoming bough,
 Drawls out, " Mi-eu, mi-ow ! "

EDITH M. THOMAS.

HOW often it happens that people are known by their least agreeable trait. The harsh catcall, " Mieu, miow ! " is the least musical of the many notes the Catbird utters. By his own song he is worthy a place with singers of highest rank. It is this that exasperates us so ; but is it so much more strange that he does not always employ his best powers than that we do not live up to our best all the time ?

The Catbird is the Mocking Bird of the north. May and June are the months when his song seems to come from the heart. Later in the season he amuses himself with a variety of vocal entertainments.

If you can read into his little picture, — slate color for the upper parts, lighter slate and gray for under parts, and black for a crown, and a tail that the owner is continually jerking, — you may surprise yourself by discovering the bird some day, for he is by no means unfamiliar with the thickets around village homes. If you should think you had done so, make quite sure by looking for a reddish patch on the under side of the tail, and a black bill.

It is said that a cat is fonder of places than of persons. Not so our little Catbird, as a story told by Miss Merriam has shown us. It is of a gentle old lady, who lived in a cottage behind an old-fashioned garden, whose rose-covered trellises, lilacs, and other shrubs and trees made it a happy spot for a resting place or a summer home both for birds and people.

The Catbird was the "comrade and favorite" of the owner of the cottage, who loved all birds and flowers. The bird would call for her in the morning, till she came to answer him with a whistle; then he would be satisfied, and would find a perch and pour out his morning song. This would be repeated many times a day in the little rests he took from his domestic duties.

It was plain that the bird was fond of her society, for when it happened one summer that the lady was away from home when he came north, and the place looked deserted, he found another place in which to build his nest. When the old lady returned, she missed her pet of many years, but as summer went on, was sure that it was he who sometimes appeared and sung to her in the garden at sunset.

All the bird students agree that the Catbird loves to have a listener.

> "Come forth!" my Catbird calls to me,
> "And hear me sing my cavatina"—

FIG. 11.—Catbird.

Lowell writes, and there are evil-minded critics who, therefore, blame the bird for vanity; but let us agree with those who love the merry song and the good-natured but capricious little singer.

This is one of the birds who has been so often on trial for his life, because his ways have been so little known. Such an individual should have one of the best of lawyers to plead his case. Several have volunteered their services, and Mr. Nehrling's testimony rests on special study. He says that the bird's usefulness as an insect destroyer is so great that the food it steals is of little importance, and that "for every cherry it takes, it eats a thousand insects."

TO A SKYLARK.

Joyous as the morning,
Thou art laughing and scorning ;
Thou hast a nest for thy love and thy rest.
Happy, happy liver,
With a soul as strong as a mountain river,
Pouring out praise to the Almighty Giver,
Joy and jollity be with us both !
Alas ! my journey, rugged and uneven,
Through prickly moors or dusty ways must wind ;
But hearing thee, or others of thy kind,
As full of gladness and as free of heaven,
I, with my fate contented, will plod on,
And hope for higher raptures, when life's day is done.

C. ROSSETTI.

NEST BUILDERS.

A S we said in an earlier lesson, the building of a nest is a matter requiring skill to plan and deftness to execute. We should do such work with hands, but a little thought will show you how unfit a bird's toes are for it.

The bill is the bird's best tool, and is, as you have

Copyright, Osprey Co., 1897.
FIG. 12. — Osprey's Nest.

learned, a chisel, a nut cracker, and a spade ; but you may have yet to learn that it is a mason's trowel, and even a needle.

Hollows in the ground, a bunch of seaweed, rude platforms of sticks are among the simplest kinds of nests. The Osprey, or Fishhawk, uses plenty of material but not much skill, and as he adds to his nest each year, it often becomes a huge pile, big enough to fill a wagon. Such a Fishhawk's nest is shown in Fig. 12.

Before I describe the more wonderful woven structure which the word nest calls up to our minds, let me speak of two more styles of building, — the holes in sand or wood, and the plastered nests of mud.

The woodpecker's chisel enables him to make a hole to order where he wants it, but many other birds, such as Bluebirds and owls, love the natural hollows in decayed limbs.

The birds that live in holes in the earth generally choose sand; you can imagine why they prefer it to clay; and river banks give them a chance to build horizontally rather than perpendicularly.

What advantage is this to them?

One bird, the Burrowing Owl, digs out a long, winding passage underground, at the end of which he has a chamber for his nest.

The mud nests, or plastered nests, are built of wet mud, taken in the bird's bill and stuck to rocks or walls of houses. Eave Swallows build a nest shaped something like a bottle, all of grains of mud. These birds gather about mud puddles in May, dipping in their bills, fluttering, twittering, lighting, and flying

off, a happy and pretty company of masons. Sometimes in very wet weather their bottle-shaped homes
crumble and fall to pieces, though they, too, know
that eaves will serve them as an umbrella.

We come now to the woven nests. Of these there
are so many and of such variety that whole books
could be written about them. Very few, however, are
more graceful and more cleverly built than our own
Oriole's; the nest is so common on our elms that we
do not realize how wonderful a work it is.

Look at a piece of felt, such as is used in making
soft hats. You see it is made of small threads closely
woven together. An Oriole's nest is like a felt pouch.
First, the Oriole fastens strong string or thread, which
he has twitched off from fibrous bark, to the twigs to
which he has chosen to hang the pouch. These serve
as a framework for the nest and must be very strong.
How does he fasten them? Just as you would, except
that he ties his knots with his beak. He makes a
loop, sticks the end through, and pulls it tight.

When the skeleton is finished, it shows the depth
and general shape of the nest. This is generally as
long as a man's hand. The bottom is rounded and
the neck narrowed a little. Now comes the weaving.
Short threads snatched from ropes, clotheslines, bits
of tow or milkweed stalks are woven in and out
through the first long threads, till the nest is so thick

and strong that it often hangs through the rain and snow of two winters after the bird has used it.

There is generally a lining in the round end on which the eggs are laid. Here the mother sits swinging in the wind till the young are hatched, and there they swing like sailor boys in a snug hammock. The leaves above them keep off the sun and rain. What bird could wish for a better home?

Few American birds are such skilful weavers as the Oriole, and none dare to hang their nests so close to the ends of twigs. The other weavers, too, generally use coarser material. Instead of fine woolen or silken threads they use roots, grass, tough barks, or even twigs; but many make wonderfully neat nests for all that. We have room to speak of only two before we leave America and hear about some foreign nest builders.

The Humming Bird's nest is as tiny as its owner; it is a little cup saddled on a twig and generally covered on the outside with the same gray lichens which grow on the twig itself. At a distance it looks like a little gray knot on a knotty bough, and most eyes, even if they rest on it, fail to see it.

The Song Sparrow and many of his family build on the ground and weave into the nest so much dry grass that the nest, half hidden under a tuft, is very hard to make out. It is only when the mother bird flies out from under our feet, as it were, that we see it and its pretty speckled eggs.

In foreign countries nests are built in much the same styles and for much the same purposes as here. When the weather is warm, of course the nests need not be so warmly built; but wherever little naked birds are born, shelter must be provided for them, and skilful bills are cutting, weaving, plastering, or even sewing to make a home for the coming young. "Sewing?" you ask, "Can a bird sew?" Yes, and the bill is its needle. The little bird who sews lives in India, and is so famous for its skill that people call it the Tailor-bird. It builds in the gardens, and several people have written about it. Here is what one gentleman says: "It makes its nest of cotton, wool, and various other soft materials, and draws together one leaf or more, generally two leaves, on each side of the nest and stitches them together with cotton, either woven by itself, or cotton thread picked up, and after passing the thread through the leaf it makes a knot at the end to fix it."

THE SWALLOWS.

How can I tell the signals and the signs
By which one heart another heart divines?

WHAT would n't we give to know what it is they are saying!—these two happy birds. I have watched pairs and companies of swallows ever since I was a child, and I cannot yet find any words that tell all that I think it is.

A year or two ago I watched a swallow family at Baker's Island, a few miles out from the North Shore of Massachusetts Bay, for a whole afternoon, just when the young ones were proving their wings and learning to fly. My piazza faced the bay from the top of a cliff, and, to keep the Island cows from going too near the edge, a single rail fence had been set up. It was from one of these rails that the start was to be made and the lesson given.

A few yards away *my* family were learning to swim, and I looked from one bit of teaching to the other, like a school inspector. I am sure I do not need to tell which class took the prize of my highest approval.

The swallow children were so near in size to their parents, that I only knew the teachers by their steady flight. There were three in the class, but I was quite

A HAPPY PAIR.

sure that one stayed in its place on the rail till almost the last moment. I tried to make myself acquainted with each, but a shout from the swimmers and bathers would draw my attention to them just at a critical time, and I could not be perfectly sure the flyers did not change places. What might a real bird student have done, if he had been interested to know the swallow's ways?

He might have searched the little island over to learn where this family went when the lesson ended, and seen what they did the next day, and the next; and if he had watched and studied with heart as well as eyes, there might have been something to give to bird-lovers in a poem or story. This is what is being done to make Bird World better understood.

THE DEPARTURE OF THE SWALLOW.

And is the swallow gone?
  Who beheld it?
  Which way sailed it?
Farewell bade it none?

No mortal saw it go:
  But who doth hear
  Its summer cheer
As it flitteth to and fro?

So the freed spirit flies!
  From its surrounding clay
  It steals away,
Like the swallow from the skies.

Whither? wherefore doth it go?
  'T is all unknown;
  We feel alone
That a void is left below.

WILLIAM HOWITT.

THE BARN SWALLOW.

WHEN a farmer builds a new barn, he plans stalls for his horses, stanchions for his cows, pens and coops for the pigs and hens, and often in the attic he cuts holes and builds little ledges for pigeons.

One guest who is quite sure to wish to come he hardly ever arranges for; but when the barn is finished and its great door stands wide open, some soft May day, the swallow flies in and out, and, perching on the wide beams under the roof, chooses a place for his nest. One farmer that I knew, thought of the swallows when he built his barn, and drove a horseshoe into a beam. Each year the swallows build a nest on this support.

Although the farmer does not exactly invite the swallows, yet nearly all farmers are glad to have them come, glad to hear them twittering on the ridgepole, glad to see them flying over the grass or up into the bright sky. "The swallows have come" is one of the best bits of news which the farmer's children can bring to their mother. It tells that summer is near, just as the first Bluebirds brought notice that winter was over.

You have read already about the mud nests of the swallows; in them the young are fed, and from them the young are coaxed by their parents to try their wings. They fly only a short distance at first, their parents flying past them, calling and showing them how easy it is. Soon the wings of the little ones grow stronger, and before many days the young are skilful enough in the air to take food from their parents while they are flying. This is one of the prettiest sights to be seen in Bird World. The parent gives a note which means "Come on, I have something for you." The young bird flies toward the old one, and as they meet

FIG. 13. — Swallow.

both fly upward, their bills touch, and the food passes from one to the other.

Wonderful wings swallows have, and wonderfully skilful and graceful is their flight. Backward and forward they pass, now with a sudden turn to the side, or a little upward one over a hedge, turning corners, slipping between men and horses, all without an effort.

When the autumn comes, the tireless wings are going to carry them to Mexico or Yucatan, where they will find old friends, Kingbirds and Bobolinks, and where new insects will taste as good to them as New England flies and gnats.

Watch a swallow hunting! Every time he turns quickly in his course, to this side or to that, another insect has passed into that wide-open mouth. Count them for a minute. The number quickly runs into the tens and twenties. Now remember that a swallow is on his feet, we should say, — on his wings, the swallows would call it, — from four o'clock in the morning to six at night, and longer in the June days. Multiply the minutes; fourteen times sixty is over eight hundred, is it not? Now, supposing he caught ten insects a minute, — and this is probably too few, — you can see that a dozen swallows would make away with a large army of insects, nearly all of which would plague the cattle, or feed upon the farmer's fruit or vegetables. The farmer has no better or more hardworking servant than the swallow. He has a good right, has he not, to the shelter, for a month or so, of the farmer's barn?

THE RED-WINGED BLACKBIRD.

Fust comes the blackbird clatterin' on tall trees,
And settlin' things in windy congresses.
LOWELL.

THERE is a little beetle that lives on water-lily leaves; and if any insect were safe from attack, you would think it might be this one. Several times, however, I have seen Red-winged Black-birds light on the leaves, as they floated on the water, and pick off the beetles. This shows us how the birds pry into every-thing, and attack our insect enemies in every part of nature.

FIG. 14. — Red-winged Blackbird.

The Red-wing is never far from the water, and often builds his nest in the bushes or sedges that grow over slow streams or ponds. In March and April he sits for hours on the top of some bush, spreading his wings to show his scarlet epaulets, and singing his loud, cheerful

"Okalee." He has many other notes and whistles; in fact the blackbird is a noisy and talkative bird, particularly at bedtime, and flocks of them make the marshes ring before they settle down to sleep. If a larger bird flies into the neighborhood, the blackbirds chase him, calling and whistling, much disturbed till he has disappeared.

The winter freezes the northern swamps, and drives the blackbirds into southern states, but the first warm March morning finds them in the north again. The males come first in great flocks, and wait for their partners. It is always a question whether the first spring bird will be a Bluebird or the Red-winged Blackbird.

Later in this book you will read about Bird Families, different kinds of birds who are related to each other, just as you have distant cousins having different names. When you come to know what birds make up the family to which the Red-winged Blackbird belongs, you will have some very interesting acquaintances. · The Bobolink, the Oriole, the lazy Cowbird, and the Meadow Lark are among them.

What different habits these creatures have! One nests in the long grass, one in tall elms, one in the swamps, and one makes no nest at all.

ABOUT BIRDS' TOES.

THE animals in Wonderland, you remember, were
always very much surprised that Alice was not
constructed just as they were themselves; in fact they
seemed rather to look down upon her because she
was different.

If Alice had met a large number of our North
American birds, I think they would have been very
scornful about the uselessness of her toes. We may
think of them as saying, "What can you do with
them?"

"Can you catch fish or mice?" "No!" Then
the hawks and owls would have turned their backs.

"Of course you can climb with them?" "No."

Then the woodpeckers would have nothing
more to say.

A fat duck would waddle up and comfort
her by saying that she
thought climbing perfectly
absurd and dangerous as
well. "But of course your
toes are webbed to help you

FIG. 15.— Duck's Foot.

swim," she might add. If you were Alice, you would
have to confess that you could not swim very well

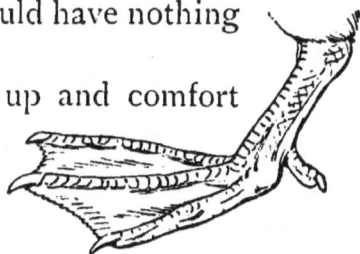

anyway, and that you used your hands more than your feet.

Neither do you scratch for seeds or worms, like the hen, nor perch, like the sparrow.

An ostrich should, at any rate, sympathize with you, for she uses her toes mainly to walk on, as you do yours.

None of the birds, however, have as many toes as

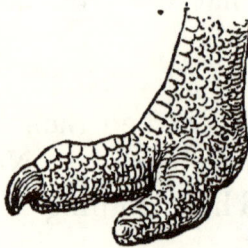

Fig. 16. — Ostrich Foot.   Fig. 17. — Foot of Song Sparrow.

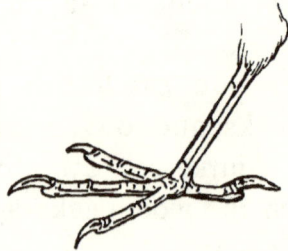

you have. Four is the largest and commonest number, usually arranged so that three toes point forward and one back. This arrangement is best suited to perch with; as one writer says, it makes the bird's foot a kind of hand, the hind toe acting like your thumb, which would help very little if it could not be brought up under your fingers.

In the hawks (see Fig. 46, p. 187) the toes are wide apart, so that a large object can be clutched and held firmly. The Fishhawk, which has to seize a very slippery prey, can turn one toe sidewise, and all the owls can do the same, so that they have a very firm grasp.

In the woodpeckers and parrots there are always two hind toes, but some other tree-climbers, like the little Brown Creeper, get up a tree just as cleverly with the usual arrangement of toes.

The little sooty brown birds, who live in your chimneys and are called Swifts, from their great speed,

FIG. 18. — Grouse Foot.   FIG. 19. — Foot of Flicker.

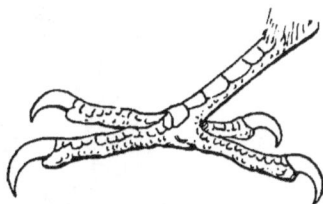

have short, weak toes which they use very little. In England there is a swift whose four toes all point forward, but the bird spends nearly all day on the wing, so that he does not need his feet for perching. Notice the short hind toes of the duck and the grouse (Figs. 15, 18), birds which flatten out the foot in walking.

The hen's hind toe, as you must know, does not touch the ground, and in some birds this toe has been used so little that it has practically disappeared.

Many birds, therefore, have only three, and generally these are all front toes.

Beside the Swift, who spends so much time in the air, there are two American birds who cannot perch in the usual way; they are Whip-poor-will and the Night Hawk.   Their toes are too short to grasp a limb stout enough to hold them, so they rest either on the ground or along, not across, a large limb.

FIG. 20. — Chimney Swift.

BOB WHITE.

HALF a mile away you can hear Bob White whistling his name, " Bob White!" " Bob White!"
The sound is so distinct that dogs, when they hear it first, show that they take it for the call of a human being. Following the sound and keeping a sharp lookout, you may find him on the fence rail, and if you creep cautiously near, you will see what a handsome bird he is.

His throat is pure white, his head marked with black and white, and his short, fat body a rich brown. Why is he whistling so clearly?

If you answer him, — for you can learn to whistle the notes almost as clearly as he does, — you may see a very fierce little Quail come flying to the spot where you are hidden, for the whistling of the Quail, like the drumming of the Grouse, is a call to his mate and a challenge to all his rivals.

Under the blackberry vines, along the wall, or in a tuft of grass in the open fields, his mate is covering, or trying to cover, a set of eggs which it would be a joy for you to see — row within row of pure white beautiful eggs, sometimes as many as twenty in a nest.

When the little ones hatch, they come out already clothed with down, and run off with their mother, like young Grouse or barnyard chickens. Their parents look after them, however, very carefully, teaching them to hide in the grass at the approach of hawks or prowling cats.

Like the Grouse, the Quail rarely leaves the fields where he was born; but, unlike the Grouse, the flock or covey, as it is called, generally keep together all winter, and instead of roosting on trees they have a very sociable habit of spending the night. The whole company squat on the ground close together, heads out, their tails forming the center of a circle. In this way they are kept warm and can be on the lookout for danger.

One winter — a sad winter for Quails — there was a heavy snow which covered the ground deeply for weeks; when it finally melted, a little circle of quail bodies was found dead. The snow had smothered and buried them as the ashes buried the people of Pompeii.

When the winter is not too severe, the Quails scratch the snow away, hunting for seeds and grain. If they have not been hunted or pursued too much, they sometimes become very tame, and come shyly into the barnyard or about the house for food.

In the summer, berries and corn and wheat that

PART OF A QUAIL FAMILY.

have dropped from the ears are crushed by their short, stout bills, and they fill out their daily bill of fare with grubs and insects.

The wings of a Quail, though strong, are short in comparison with the weight of his body. They are also somewhat concave, like the inner side of a watch crystal, so that when the bird flies the rapid strokes and the shape of the wing make a loud whirring sound.

Quails are not as common as they once were. Too many of them, instead of wandering about the pastures, hang in the markets, their pretty feathers soiled and a little stain of blood telling the story of their death ; but if the extermination were to become complete, the only ones to be benefited would be such real enemies to our crops as the potato beetle and the cutworm. In Wisconsin they were brought back by a state law, as song birds were said to be in Killingworth.

AUDUBON AND THE PHŒBES.

A PAIR of Phœbes once built in a cave near Audubon's house. He visited them so often, and was so careful not to frighten them, that they finally paid no more heed to his presence than if he had been a post. He was therefore able to learn much about their manner of life; he found out how often eggs were laid, and how long the female sat upon them. As the young grew up he handled them frequently, so that they, too, grew accustomed to him.

As they grew older he tied bits of thread to their legs, but these they always pulled off. When, however, they became so used to the threads that they allowed them to remain on their legs, Audubon wound a silver thread on the leg of each, "loose enough not to hurt" them, "but so fastened that no exertion of the birds could remove it." Soon the birds left the nest and in the autumn went south.

The next spring Audubon hunted up all the Phœbe's nests in the neighborhood and caught the females as they sat upon the nest. Do you not imagine that he was pleased to find that on the legs of two birds was a light, silver thread?

HOW YOUNG BIRDS GET FED.

ONE afternoon in July I watched six little Barn Swallows sitting on the roof of a barn. They had evidently left their nest only a few days before, but their wings were already strong enough to carry them back to the roof if they fluttered off.

Soon the father approached, and was greeted by six gaping mouths. The little bird sitting nearest him got the mouthful, and an instant later got another from the mother. Six times in succession he was fed, neither parent regarding the five other yellow throats.

This seemed unfair, and foolish as well. I thought little birds must be starved one day and fed too full the next. I waited a few moments and the mystery was solved. The little fellow who had been getting so much soon had all he wanted. The next time the parents came his mouth was shut, and one of the other five got the mouthful.

When a cat or a dog has had enough, he stops eating. It must be so with little birds; when one has had enough, he shuts his mouth and eyes and dozes while his brothers and sisters get their meal. I fear, though, that when there are six mouths to fill, the last is hardly closed before the first opens again.

BY carpentering, by painting, by selling goods,—
by so many different kinds of work that it would
be hard to make a list of them all,—your fathers
provide your daily food.

Long ago, in the old forests of England or Germany, our ancestors got their own food by hunting,
fishing, keeping cattle, and by a little farming. To-
day this work is done for us, but the birds have still
to do their foraging for themselves.

Birds eat the things which you eat, and besides
have the whole insect world to hunt in. You can
often tell by a bird's appearance what he eats, and
when you have found that out, you can generally tell
where he will choose to live, and what many of his
habits of life are. When you see the wide mouth of
a swallow, and his long, slender wings, you will decide
that if any bird could catch the hosts of flies, gnats,
and beetles that fill the air in summer, certainly the
swallow should be well fitted for such hunting. When
you remember that hard frosts kill these flying insects,
you will feel sure that you will find no swallows here
in winter. The long, sharp bill of a heron, and his
long, naked feet seem well fitted for spearing frogs

BLACK-THROATED GREEN WARBLERS.

and fish in shallow water.   Herons must therefore live
near water, and in winter go where the swamps are
not frozen.

Such birds as Crows eat many kinds of food; whatever they can get, in fact.   In spring the farmer's
corn tastes sweet to them, but the grubs and beetles
are good food, too, and they find that no one will
shoot them for taking the grubs, while eating corn
means taking some risk.   In fall and winter, nuts are
also added to the Crow's bill of fare.   Near the sea-
shore, dead fish and other sea animals which are
found on the shore vary the food in winter.   I am
ashamed to say that eggs, and even young birds, are
sometimes devoured by the Crow.   When a bird is
so easily pleased, and has such a wide choice, he can
stay all the year round.

Seed-eating birds, like the sparrows, can find seeds
on the weeds and grasses even in winter, and the little
bark inspectors find eggs, cocoons, and sleepy beetles
in the cracks of the bark, so that winter does not
frighten them away.   Many of the sea birds, especially
the divers, can find fish or shellfish in the winter sea,
where it does not freeze over.

Did you ever think why the Pine Warbler loved the
pines, and the Summer Yellowbird preferred the
willows?   Not because either of them eats the seeds
or leaves of these trees, but because in them each

finds the insects he has learned to catch. Sometimes
a bird's food depends so largely on a certain tree that
he will have to leave a town, if these trees are all cut
down.

Sometimes birds have found a certain kind of food
or a way of getting food so different from that of any
other bird that their bills or feet have gradually
changed, and they have become more and more
dependent on this way of getting their living. The
woodpecker's tongue is a long, hooked brush, with
which he rakes out grubs from deep holes, the Humming Bird's tongue is a tube through which he sucks
honey, and the Flamingo's bill is a sieve through
which he strains muddy water as a whale strains the
sea water through his whalebone meshes.

You could find many stories about the strange food
or feeding habits of birds. First, however, look about
you, if you can, and find out what the birds that are
your own neighbors eat, and how they get it. Take
the common birds, the Robin, the Chipping Sparrow,
the Kingbird, and the Gull, and watch them till you
see them getting and eating their dinner. Then you
will be all the more interested in the interesting
stories you will find in the books. You will learn,
too, what patience and sharp sight people come
to have who watch birds and find out all their
secrets.

WHEN A BIRD CHANGES HIS CLOTHES.

D O you know how important the masts of a sailing ship are? If they are broken, the ship is helpless. It drifts about wherever the wind blows it.

A bird's wing and tail feathers are as important for its safety as the mast and sails of a ship. The strong, powerful quill feathers enable it to fly rapidly through the air to get its food and to avoid its enemies. It is important that the feathers of both wings should be uninjured, for the bird would be unable to guide its flight if one wing were much less strong than the other.

Feathers get worn by use, some even get broken, and if the bird could not replace them it would have hard work, after a year or two, to make the old weatherworn ones do their work.

Nature, however, provides the birds with a new suit of clothes every year. After the young are hatched, when the old birds no longer need their swiftness and strength to get the daily food for their children, the feathers of almost all birds begin to drop out; not at once, for that would leave the bird naked and helpless, but gradually and, in the case of the wing feathers, fairly evenly. As fast as the feathers drop out others grow out to take their places, and in a month or so the bird has a new suit of fine strong feathers, all ready to carry him to his distant winter home.

With many of the birds of the Duck and Goose family, the moulting goes on so quickly that the bird has scarcely enough feathers to enable him to fly. He hides during these unhappy weeks in distant swamps, hoping that no enemy will attack him till he is ready to fly again. He must feel like a cripple and try his wings impatiently, longing for the day when he can be off again through the air.

In the case of many gay-colored male birds, this summer moult leaves them very shabby-looking. The Bobolink loses all his gay black and white, and comes out in August in brown and yellowish, like his wife and children. He probably does not feel so proud of his good looks as before, but I think he is safer. The black and white was so bright that his enemies could easily see him, but now he can slip away among the brown grasses and hardly be noticed.

Many male birds are not content with one suit of feathers a year. They have to have another new suit, or part of one; in the spring, and of the gayest colors and feathers. Red and blue and yellow appear on the shoulders, in the tail, on the head, neck, and breast, in patches, bars, bands, streaks, in fact in every way that can make the bird attractive. The little fellows know very well what a fine appearance they now make. If there is any bit of color that does not show well, they take pains to bow or bend, or to spread wing or tail to display it. All these bright feathers are moulted again and the winter suit put on. So the suits change with the seasons, till the little life is ended.

———

The Humming Birds are a perpetual pleasure. I shall never forget the surprise of joy the first time one alighted on my sleeve and rested, as much at home as if I were a stick or harmless twig.

Sparrows and Nuthatches had often alighted on my head as I stood musing over my flowers, but to have this tiny spark of brilliant life come to anchor, as it were, on anything so earthly as my arm was indeed a nine days' wonder. Now it has grown to be an old story, but it is never any less delightful.— CELIA THAXTER, *An Island Garden.*

EVERY boy or girl who knows the winter woods has seen, hanging from the forked twigs of bushes or low trees, shallow, cup-shaped nests like that in the picture.

These woodland nests are generally built by the Red-eyed Vireo, a bird whose enticing song and gentle manners soon win affection, if one learns to know him. The nest in the picture, however, is that of his cousin, the Yellow-throated Vireo, whose disposition is even more confiding than the Red-eye's.

I have always liked Yellow-throated Vireos, because of the careless, confident way in which the male sings on the nest; and when a pair of these vireos appeared last May in an apple tree just outside my dining-room window, I was prepared to give them a very cordial welcome. I had no idea, however, when the female finally selected a twig and fell to weaving, how important a member of our household she would become, and what charming associations she was destined to weave about the tree.

It was the seventeenth of May when she began the nest. By night it seemed to me finished, but to her trained eye it was still insecure. All the next morning she kept at work, and at noon I could easily see that the walls were much thicker and more smoothly covered.

On the twenty-second of May there was one egg in the nest; the next morning, a second. On the twenty-sixth I placed a short ladder against the tree, so that when I climbed it my head was level with the nest and within two feet of it.

I climbed the ladder twice, to accustom the bird to her strange visitor, and the third time I offered her a cankerworm. She took it, but flew off with it.

The next morning I made the fourth ascent of the ladder and offered the vireo a large black ant, which I caught on the tree itself. She swallowed it without leaving the nest, and a dozen more disappeared as quickly as I could give them to her. These black ants were evidently considered very choice food, and as there were large colonies of them in the hollows of the tree, there was always a busy line following up or down the limb against which the ladder rested. The simplest way, therefore, to feed my friend was to stand on the ladder, waylay each passing ant and offer it to her.

The next morning, on my fifth ascent, she again ate freely from my hand and from my lips. She even left her eggs and perched on the edge of the nest, reaching forward if I held the ant too far from her;

and when I had desolated the highway of ants and was descending the ladder, she flew from the limb below the nest to the top rung of the ladder, and after I fed her there, to the next rung, following me some distance. The male, whom I soon learned to distinguish by the richer yellow of his throat, was naturally aroused and indignant at this intrusion. While his mate was eating peacefully from my hand, he flew backward and forward close to my head, uttering a harsh, scolding note, which I never heard from the female.

In about a week after he first witnessed the performance, the male became, to a certain extent, reconciled to his wife's strange conduct. He did not dart at my head so often, and he developed a habit which gave me a much higher opinion of his character, — flying to the nest when the female followed me and keeping the eggs warm during her absence.

Once, indeed, while I was feeding her on the nest, some time after he had grown used to me, I heard him scolding more violently than ever. I wondered at his renewed vigilance, till I saw that he was watching, not me, but a male vireo. His anger at my intrusion had been somewhat modified by astonishment, but the presence of another bird was an occurrence he understood and felt competent to deal with.

The male never fed from my hand, although he

often remained in the nest until I came very near. I knew him at once by his retracted head and angry eyes. The female's head was always extended to see what I was bringing her, and her eyes were intelligent and gentle.

He was a true barbarian, I fear, but I learned to respect him thoroughly. He defended his home and family as well as he could, and he was extremely active, a little later, in feeding the young. I told my friends, of course, of the rare friendship which I had formed, and several came to see the vireo eat from my hand. Not only did their presence under the tree seem to make no difference in her appetite, but when one of them climbed the ladder I had to admit that she took food from his hand as readily as she had from mine. At no time did she discriminate between her admirers. Any one who brought black ants was welcome.

FIG. 21.— Yellow-throated Vireo.

On the twenty-eighth of May I put her courage to

a severe test.   She was standing on the edge of the
nest, the better to reach for the food which I offered
her, and her composure was so great and my hand so
near, that I ventured to close it over her and to carry
her toward me.

She did not seem alarmed at this strange experience; her heart was not beating at a rapid rate, but I

FIG. 22.— Vireo and Nest.

think the position was too unusual to be comfortable.
She seemed pleased to be put down, although she
remained where I placed her and continued her
meal.

If I put an ant on the palm of my hand, she preferred to hover or to fly over and take the ant on the
wing; yet on the third of June I induced her to perch
on my finger.

I managed this by putting a box containing ants in the palm of my hand, but letting it show between my fingers. She wanted the ants and saw only one way to get at them. She alighted, therefore, on my finger and thrust her bill down into the box. She also learned to eat from the box placed upon my head.

In order to photograph the bird in these characteristic positions, we had to do an amount of climbing and cutting in the tree, which was in itself a severe test of her composure. The camera, too, on its tripod, was tied in place only a foot or two away, and remained there night and day, covered by a black cloth; but neither this strange object nor the removal of twigs and branches all around the nest seemed to disturb the vireo in the least.

By the eighteenth of June the young were hatched, and as soon as they no longer needed the protection of her body, the mother treated herself to long and well-earned absences. Once she was away so long that I became greatly worried about her, but she returned at length, and ate once more, the last time, from my hand.

She unconsciously gave me cause, during this last interview, to think of her a little more constantly than I liked. While I looked up at her as she fed, there fell into my eye a fragment of the ant she was eating

—an experience that forbids me to recommend formic acid as an eye lotion.

But I forgave her, of course, and, as I say, this was the last I saw of her. At the end of two days I went away for the summer. When I returned, in September, the well-worn nest was all that I could connect with the family I had watched. Often when I look at it I think of its brave architect and builder. I remember how helpless her little body felt in my hand, and I wonder what long journeys she is making now.

Most of all, I wonder whether she will escape all' the perils of the way and return to me next spring. The chances are many that I shall not see my vireo again, but if she returns next May the warmest welcome and the largest ants will be waiting for her.

————

Redstarts, like all little birds, are "feathered appetites," and this means the destruction of innumerable insects, health of shade trees, and the perfecting of flowers.—C. C. ABBOTT.

> The happy birds that change their sky
> To build and brood ; that live their life
> From land to land.
>> TENNYSON'S *In Memoriam.*

BIRD PASSPORTS.

DO you know what a passport is?

In all parts of our country orderly persons may move about freely without exciting suspicion. In countries differently governed stricter rules prevail, and circumstances are liable to arise in which it is necessary to be quickly and easily identified, and to have the protection of one's own country.

If none of you have done so, many of your parents have had to pass, during a single summer, through France, Germany, Italy, Switzerland, if not through cities of Austria, Turkey, Russia, and perhaps countries of Asia and Africa. The form of protection in such cases is a written passport signed by one of the highest officers of our government. On the following page is a copy of such a passport.

If any wrong should come to one holding this paper, he can appeal to his government to see that it is righted, as far as is possible; and if he himself does violence or injury, his government is made responsible for his wrongdoing.

You can see that such a paper must not be transferred from person to person. To make sure that the holder of it is the rightful owner, he is carefully described in the document, as you see.

UNITED STATES · AMERICA

DEPARTMENT · STATE

To all to whom these presents shall come · Greeting:

I the undersigned, Secretary of State of the United States of America,
hereby request all whom it may concern, to permit

_____ a Citizen of the United States accompanied
by his wife and two minor children safely
and freely to pass and in case of need to give
him all lawful Aid and Protection.

Description

Age 58 Years _____
Stature 6 Feet 2 Inches Eng.
Forehead high _____
Eyes blue _____
Nose regular _____
Mouth small _____
Chin round _____
Hair grey _____
Complexion fair _____
Face beard _____

Signature of the Bearer

_____

[Seal]

Given under my hand and the
Seal of the Department of State,
at the City of Washington,
the 8 th day of August
in the year 1898, and of the
Independence of the United States
the one hundred and twenty third

William R. Day

"But what," you ask, " has this to do with birds? "
Only this: the birds are the greatest travelers in the
world. They must go, in the different seasons of the
year, where the food they need is most plentiful. If
they do not have to "sow or reap or gather into
barns," it is also true that they must glean and forage
day by day to meet their needs. They are happiest
in summer time in northern latitudes; but when frost
comes and the insects are safe in winter cocoons, they
must go where summer heat lasts the long year
through. Traveling is not so much a pastime as a
necessity.

Going high over our heads, they do not ask our
leave. Their frequent way stations are the tree tops,
the marsh grasses, and all sorts of open or hidden
ways. Some go singing, like the old-time Troubadours.

The migration of different kinds of birds is becom-
ing better known every year, and as they are interesting visitors we are all glad to know when they will
come our way, and how we may know them as they
pass. While they accept our hospitality without ask-
ing for it, with very few exceptions (hardly worthy
to be named), they are of the greatest service to us.
Longfellow's " Birds of Killingworth " tells what this
service is.

Now, I am sure you can see how it is that an exact
description of every known bird would be of great use

for many different reasons. You and I would be glad to have so good a statement of the birds we wish to know that when we see a bird we may be helped in finding out what bird it is. And students who wish to know the family relations of different birds are glad of strict bird passports for that purpose. Those who have in times past shot birds, thinking they would get better crops, need to learn what birds have deserved their thanks instead.

If we think of this, we shall find more pleasure in the bird books written for older students, which have seemed to contain nothing but dull statements. We shall prize them as we do dictionaries.

There is another idea connected with this matter of passports. As you grow older and study birds for yourselves, you will wish to compare what you learn with what others know. To do this well and easily you must be able to make out the passports, or descriptions, which are used in bird study.

Many birds are so much alike that it often requires quite a full description to enable any one who knows to tell which of several birds you have in mind. It is the object of this lesson to start you in making descriptions for yourselves, as well as in using those of other people.

THE BIRD OF MANY NAMES.

IN our world we are apt to express an opinion of persons who in different places pass under different names. To appear in full wedding suit of three striking colors in New England in May and June, then to don a snuffy brown traveling suit under the names of Reed and Rice in different localities of the south, and in Cuba to assume a foreign name, while at least two other names are held in good faith by people somewhere else, would need explanation.

FIG. 23. — Bobolink.

But we know little of the use of names in Bird World. A few birds tell us plainly what they like to be called: Whip-poor-will, Bob White, Chickadee; for the most part we have put our own, often very stupid, names upon them.

A Bobolink is a much-beloved bird in New England. It would seem a crime against nature to shoot him, and there would be no motive save to enrich a museum or milliner's window.

But in South Carolina or Georgia a farmer might be pardoned for finding a way to save his crops from the Rice Birds, and if he, for his part, gets morsels for his table, he would not be half paid for the young rice grains that the great flocks of passing birds devour.

By the time those that have escaped the perils of gunners reach Central America, they are said to be dainty eating as Butter Birds for those whose consciences let them secure them, and we cannot blame the people much, since the birds keep their gay holiday, wear their bright plumage, sing their gay songs with us, and make themselves much less attractive in the land of their winter exile.

The female bird wears only the yellowish brown with dashes of light and dark on wings, tail, and back.

Modest and shy as a nun is she,
Pretty and quiet, with plain brown wings,
Passing at home a patient life,
Broods in the grass while her husband sings,
          " Bob-o-link, Bob-o-link,
              Spink, Spank, Spink."

THE BOBOLINK.

BOBOLINK! that in the meadow,
  Or beneath the orchard's shadow,
Keepest up a constant rattle
Joyous as my children's prattle,
Welcome to the north again!
Welcome to mine ear thy strain,
Welcome to mine eye the sight
Of thy buff, thy black, and white.
Brighter plumes may greet the sun
By the banks of Amazon;
Sweeter tones may weave the spell
Of enchanting Philomel;
But the tropic bird would fail,
And the English nightingale,
If we should compare their worth
With thine endless, gushing mirth.

A single note, so sweet and low,
Like a full heart's overflow,
Forms the prelude; but the strain
Gives us no such tone again,
For the wild and saucy song
Leaps and skips the notes among,

With such quick and sportive play,
Ne'er was madder, merrier lay.

Nor care nor fear thy bosom knows;
For thee a tempest never blows;
But when our northern summer 's o'er,
By Delaware's or Schuylkill's shore
The wild rice lifts its airy head,
And royal feasts for thee are spread.
And when the winter threatens there,
Thy tireless wings yet own no fear,
But bear thee to more southern coasts,
Far beyond the reach of frosts.

Bobolink! still may thy gladness
Take from me all taints of sadness;
Fill my soul with trust unshaken
In that Being who has taken
Care for every living thing
In summer, winter, fall, and spring.

THOMAS HILL.

If I were a bird, in building my nest, I should follow the example of the Bobolink, placing it in the
midst of a broad meadow, where there was no spear
of grass, or flower, or growth unlike another to mark
its site. — BURROUGHS.

GYPSY BIRDS.

THERE are many land birds whose whole lives are passed almost in the same spot, and others that make great journeys twice a year; both kinds, however, the stay-at-homes as well as the travelers, are regular in their habits.

You can tell where to find them or when to expect them, sometimes almost to a day. Orioles, for instance, reach Massachusetts, almost every year, in the first week of May and leave in the last week of August.

Regular habits like these do not suit gypsies nor the Gypsy Birds; they wander from place to place wherever they find the food they like. Sometimes they appear in the fall in great numbers, and stay through the winter and late into the spring. The next year and the next they are absent; perhaps ten years elapse before they revisit the place.

The best known of the gypsy birds are the Cross-bills, whose strange pair of scissors you find among the bird bills illustrated on page 197. The handsomest gypsies in Bird World are the Pine Grosbeaks; the most lovable ones are the Linnets. All these live in the far north, where snow lies on the ground for the greater part of the year, in the great pine and spruce forests, or still further north where the white birches grow, and the owls and foxes are white as the white snow.

No one knows when to expect these gypsies. Any winter they may appear; the rosy-colored Linnets, in flocks of hundreds, light on the birches and scatter the seed-wings over the snow. The Crossbills go to the spruce cones for their seeds, and the Grosbeaks eat, I am sorry to say, not only the seeds but the buds as well. However, they come so rarely that they do little harm, and they are so beautiful and so tame that every one welcomes them.

Probably if you were to put on your snowshoes and travel far northward when you heard that these birds had come, till you should come to the great forests where they were born, you would discover why they had come south.

Not that they fear the cold, for they often live happily where the thermometer goes down to 30° below zero. No, you would look at the trees, and if you saw that the birches, for some reason, had had a poor crop of seeds, as sometimes the apple tree's crop fails, or that there were few cones on the spruces, you would make up your mind that the gypsy birds had wandered south for food.

DO you know what a foster-mother is?
If you have read Hans Andersen's famous story,
The Ugly Duckling, you will remember that the
duck mother found a strange egg in her nest, and
when it hatched, the bird that came out was larger by
half than her own ducklings. So ugly and awkward
it was that all the creatures in the farmyard pecked
at it. The good mother, though she was ashamed of
it, tried to protect it, and treated it kindly.

Birds which hatch eggs which they did not themselves lay are called foster-mothers, and there are
more of them in Bird World than most people
suppose.

If you are walking in the fields, you may come
across a strange sight, — a young bird, considerably
larger than a sparrow, squatting on the ground with
beak wide open and wings hanging down. In a
moment he will squall loudly, and then run a few
steps in the direction of a smaller bird which is busily
hunting for insects or grubs. When the smaller bird
finds something, she hurries to the lazy youngster
and gives it to him; but he has hardly swallowed
it before his mouth is open for more. He gives his

little foster-mother no peace, and you wonder she is
not utterly worn out. If you caught the two birds
and looked at their passports, you could find very
little close family resemblance, and would feel sure
that the young bird was no true child of the other.

But where are the bird's own brood? Did she
have none, and has she adopted an orphan?   ,

This is the sad part of the story, for even in Bird
World there are some very rascally characters, it
would seem, and the truth about them must be told.
The little Vireo or Redstart had built her nest and
laid her eggs in it; but one morning, while she had
left it for a moment to get food, a larger bird had
come sneaking through the bushes and had dropped
her own big egg into the nest, among the pretty little
ones that really belonged there.

When the Vireo or Redstart came back, she expected
to settle herself comfortably on the nest, with her bill
and tail and little black eye just showing over the
edge, to brood and brood all the long day. What's
to be done? She calls in great excitement to her
mate, and the pair have a long consultation, but they
are not strong to throw the egg out, and if they desert
the nest their own precious eggs will never hatch, so
they decide to make the best of it, not knowing that
what they call best is really the very worst. For, as
soon as the mother settles down, the big egg gets all

the warmth of her body, and hatches a day or two before the others, or if they hatch at the same time, the big stranger needs so much more food that the real children are in danger of being but half fed.

It is a sad story, is it not? The lazy Cowbird mother shirks all the work which we praise birds for doing. She makes no nest, she takes no pains to feed and protect her young. All her life she simply eats and sleeps and looks about her for some smaller bird whom she can deceive.

The pleasant part of the story is the kindness of the poor Redstart mother to her foster-child. She has probably lost her own brood, but instead of pecking the stranger to death, she feeds him, working day after day over him till he is big enough to fly away, which he does without a word of thanks.

Do you wonder how the Cowbird came by so odd a name? Like most bird names, some habit of the bird suggested it. These birds are often seen in small flocks following cattle in pastures. It does not require great shrewdness to guess that it is not the cows, but the insects to be found upon them in warm weather, that attract the birds. If they do service to the cattle, we are glad to give them credit, but it is said, on good authority, that every Cowbird means the loss of a whole brood of Redstarts, Yellow Warblers, Vireos, or other birds of which we cannot have too many.

TWO FATHER BIRDS.

YOU have discovered before now that birds, like people, have very different habits and characters. Even in the birds about you, the difference between a lazy Cowbird mother and such a careful, loving parent as the Grouse is very noticeable.

The birds I am going now to tell you about are natives of countries far from America. One is well known to you; some of you have perhaps seen an Ostrich at a circus. The other is not nearly so famous, but he is almost as interesting. He belongs to the sandpiper family, and is called the Ruff.

The Ruff's name comes probably from a wonderful collar of feathers which grow each spring beneath and around his throat. They are so thick that they form a shield, and the bird uses them as such. The Ruffs choose places to which they return each night simply to fence with their bills. These bills are long but not very sharp, so that they never injure each other, but they fight as fiercely as if they meant to kill one another. Many male birds of other kinds fight in the breeding season, but with the Ruffs it seems to be merely for the sake of fighting, for they keep it up even after the female is sitting on her eggs. Instead of keeping near her, as many males do, to protect her and the nest from enemies, the Ruff spends his time with the other males, fighting continual duels, until the summer comes. Then his collar gradually drops off, and the males that have been fighting all the spring go off together in peaceful flocks.

The male Ostrich has a very different character from the quarrelsome and neglectful Ruff. The Ostrich, like our barnyard rooster, has several hens. All lay eggs in the same nest, which is nothing but a pit scraped out in the sand. In this

FIG. 24. — The Ruff.

sometimes thirty eggs are laid. Every night the male Ostrich broods on this great pile. If the young are threatened, the male defends them, or tries to lead the enemy astray by pretending that he is wounded or lame, just as the mother Grouse does here.

Of the two fathers, the Ruff is by far the handsomer. The bare red neck of the Ostrich is ugly enough, but uglier when compared with the Ruff's fine collar. Ask their wives, however, about it, and perhaps they will say, " Handsome is that handsome does."

BORN IN A BOAT.

THERE is no bird more skilful in diving than the Grebe. He has a trick of sinking out of sight which is so wonderful that you hardly believe that the bird has been in. sight at all. Or if he is in a hurry he turns head over heels like a duck, and then the game is to guess where he will come up. It may be to the right, to the left, far or near, and sometimes you will think he has never come up at all. If a Grebe ' is fired at, he will start at the flash of the powder and be safe under water before the shot reaches the spot where he was.

When the mother Grebe is swimming about with her little ones, teaching them to dive after minnows and bolt them down whole, she will often take them for a very curious ride. They get on her back, grasp her feathers tightly with their feet, and she dives while they hold bravely on. I watched a mother once who had only a single chick, though the family is usually large. When the pair saw me, the little fellow swam to his mother and she prepared to take him down in the usual way. But either she went too fast or he lost his hold, for when she disappeared he was washed off, and sat there bobbing up and down on the ripple she had left, turning about like a walnut shell, the picture of helplessness and loneliness.

I wonder what the poor mother thought when she came up in some quiet spot and found that her baby had been lost. She did not return while I waited, but I have no doubt they were soon reunited, and very glad she must have been that it was only a wave that had carried him off, and not a snake or a pickerel.

But you are waiting to hear about the boat in which he was born. It does n't sail about, it is true, but it is really a boat at anchor.

The mother Grebe makes a nest of coarse reeds woven together. The nest is fastened to reeds that are growing out of the water, and often rests upon the water. It gets water soaked, of course, but the shell, with its lining of skin, keeps the moisture out. The eggs are kept warm by the mother bird, and warm moisture does not keep the young from hatching.

Grebes are most graceful in the water, but seem out of place on shore. Their feet are placed so far back in their bodies that they can hardly walk or stand.

HOW THE WOOD DUCK GETS HER YOUNG
TO THE WATER.

A VERY interesting story it would make to describe all the modes by which young children and animals are carried from place to place by their parents. The Indian papoose travels long distances on its mother's back; young opossums also ride on their mothers' backs, but to get a firmer hold wind their little tails round that of their mother. The mother kangaroo keeps her little children in a pouch or fold of her skin; little toads, of one kind, live in holes in their mother's back.

Young birds do little traveling before they learn to use their wings or legs. The Wood Duck, however, builds her nest in the hollow of a tree, and when the young ducks hatch, she wishes, like all other ducks, to introduce them at once to the water. You have seen a mother cat carry her kittens in her mouth. She holds them tight, but does not hurt them. So the Wood Duck takes her downy little ducklings with her broad bill and flies to the ground. Her family is large; over a dozen trips are sometimes needed from the nest to the ground. Then the procession starts off for the water, and the little ducks paddle off as easily as if they had not been born on land.

THE GREAT CARAVAN ROUTE.

YOU remember that the old Grouse boasted that he kept warm and well fed even when the ground was frozen and covered with snow. If you were to walk through his woods in January, you would find tracks in the snow, and at last he would start up from under the bushes ahead of you, with a whirr that would frighten you the first time you heard it. And when he had flown off, how silent the woods would be! You might walk for miles and meet less than half a dozen birds.

In spring the edges of the woods and the fields near by would ring with bird music, but now a few lisping notes from the Kinglets and Chickadees, the scream of a Blue Jay, or the caw of a Crow would be the only sounds made by birds.

Not quite the only ones, after all, for the little Downy Woodpecker pays his visits to the grubs at all seasons, and wakes them from their winter sleep by knocking politely at their doors.

Where have the birds gone? Where is the Oven-bird, and the Tanager? Where are the thrushes and the vireos?

It is easy to tell you where they are, but much harder to say how they got there. If you wished to

visit the islands where these birds winter, the forests
where flowers always bloom and insects are never
killed by frost, you must go either by train to Florida, and then cross by steamer from Tampa Bay to
Havana, or you can take other steamers which sail
directly from Boston, New York, and other eastern
cities to the West Indies. Unless you live on some
main line, you will have first to travel a shorter or
longer distance, as the case may be, by side lines,
which bring you to the big city where the steamers
or the fast express trains start. The birds, as you
know, can take neither train nor boat. How is it
they are in New England in September, and in
November already in Cuba?

You may have read how from Samarcand or
Irkutsk the lines of camels start for a long and difficult journey across the desert. Many fall exhausted
by the way, or are attacked and killed by highway-
men. Merchants, often of different tribes, form a
company for mutual protection. In the African
deserts the caravans find pleasant spots called oases,
where they halt to refresh themselves from the wells
or springs, and to rest a little before they take up
their journeying again.

The birds, too, form caravans before they start on
their long journeys in the fall. They have their
meeting places where different tribes assemble. They

are the ships of the air as the camels are ships of the desert.

Often the caravan is overtaken by a storm and many birds die, or, when they are resting in some friendly thicket or grove, robbers in the shape of hawks attack them. It is by no means an easy journey, and yet, by far the larger part of the birds that are with us in the summer make it not once but twice a year.

Some birds prefer to travel by day, and these have no difficulty in finding the way. Many of you have heard in the pleasant autumn days, far above, the honk of the wild geese, and you can imagine that the old goose, at the head of the great V-shaped line, can find, from his great height, landmarks in rivers and lakes which he has passed before and remembers.

But most of the birds go by night — if you think of the robber hawks you will guess why — and for them the journey is far harder. But even at night, if it is clear, ponds shine and the mountains loom up dark and large, and the old birds that have been that way before find landmarks to steer by.

They call from time to time, and the rest of the caravan coming behind answer them. On they fly till dawn, when they drop down, tired and hungry, to rest through the day, and perhaps for several days, before they take another night journey.

It is while they are resting in this way in the thickets, or perhaps in the orchards or gardens of the towns, that men who are fond of birds discover them and learn how they are getting on in their journeys. It may come about some time that a telegram may be sent to the daily papers saying that such and such birds are at Charleston or Savannah or Tampa. This would please many readers, but we must wait till we are much more kindhearted than many people are now, or it would be no kindness to the birds.

If you were to go out some morning in September and find strange birds in your garden scratching under the currant bushes, or merely hiding and resting, and the next morning find them missing, you would know that your city or town was on the great caravan route from the frozen north to the sunny south.

As for myself, I am turned hammock contractor for the Orioles, taking my pay in " notes." I throw strings out of the window and they snap at them at once. They sit in the cherry tree hard by and warble, " Hurry up, hurry up!" I never found out before just what they said. But if you listen you will find that this is what they first say. — LOWELL.

BIRD WORLD IN WINTER.

W E will go well out of city or village, and, as
birds are creatures of habit, we will take
counsel of some one whose long acquaintance with
them has let him into their secrets, to know where to
find them.

Are we afraid to venture out directly after a storm?
The way to some partial clearing in the woods may
be rough, but where tiny birds can be merry and
light-hearted we will not mind if the frost stings our
ears and finger-tips.

The woods in this case are in Ohio, and the one to
tell us of them is Mr. Leander S. Keyser. The first
sound that echoes through the woods is the vigorous
bugle of the hardy Carolina Wren. The most of the
winter birds go in straggling flocks, but this little
hero of many storms is apt to be alone.

Mr. Chapman calls this restless, excitable bird a
"feathered Jack-in-a-box," bobbing about, gesticulating
with his expressive tail, and seldom in sight more
than a minute at a time. He sings as he goes, with
a vocabulary so rich he has been called the Mocking
Wren.

How can we help shivering to see a little commu-
nity of Tree Sparrows holding a winter carnival in

the new-fallen snow? When once we have had their tracks or footprints pointed out to us, we may be sure we shall find them in our own neighborhoods also in winter. In the wildest wind and snow flurries the Tree Sparrows will keep up their cheerful chirp, while they flit about on the snow as if it were down, picking seeds from grass stems and weed stalks. Emerson defines a weed as a plant man has not yet found a use for. We and the sparrows have found a use for weeds.

Sometimes the tracks showed that the birds had taken a bite, as it were, and then had flitted across the snow to another spot; deepened hollows showed where they had wallowed in the drifts for mere fun, as boys delight to do. Brave little sparrows, you are better comrades than we thought.

"I have seen birds," says Mr. Keyser, "taking pool-baths, shower-baths, dew-baths, and dust-baths. Who will say they never take a snow-bath?"

Here in the very middle of winter we are watching a Junco. He finds a feast of juicy berries on the dog-wood tree, picks one, dashes down into the snow and nibbles it, then flings the seed away, standing leg-deep in ice crystals until he has eaten it up. The rest of the birds eat their berries where they find them on the trees. Tree Sparrows come to the dogberry tree also, but they reject the pulp and bore the pit for

WINTER LIFE.

KINGLETS.   A BROWN CREEPER.

its tiny kernel, while Robins, Bluebirds, and the rest swallow the berry whole when they come to it.

One little story that Mr. Keyser tells shall end our January visit. It is about a Junco.

"From a cornfield I witnessed a little scene that filled me with delight. At some distance I perceived a snowbird eating seeds from the raceme of a tall weed, which bent over in a graceful arch beneath its dainty burden. I climbed the fence and crept cautiously nearer to get a better view of the little diner-out. What kind of a discovery do you suppose I made? I could scarcely believe my eyes.

"There beneath the weed, hopping about on the snow, were a Tree Sparrow and a Junco, picking up the seeds that their companion above was shaking down. It was such a pretty little comedy that I laughed aloud for pure delight. It seemed for all the world like a boy in an apple tree shaking down the mellow fruit for his playmates, who were gathering it from the ground as it fell. Farther on in the woods I saw a Junco dart up to a weed too small to afford him a comfortable perch, give it a shake which would bring down a quantity of seeds, and then flit below and eat them from the white tablecloth."

BIRD LODGINGS IN WINTER.

WE have been told what Robins do at night; but Robindom is but a small part of Bird World. It does not matter much on summer nights, but in early February and March, or even in the storms of April and May, we might rest better if we knew just how the birds we were so glad to see in the morning sunshine were faring now that the sun has gone down.

It is quite plain that nothing troubles a bird much but fear of enemies and scarcity of food. If he can keep the little heart within him warm and safe, he will make a merry life. Since it was found out what Robins do, bird students have been watching late and rising before dawn to solve the kindly problem of birds' night quarters.

The first thought is that they would be in bushes and trees; but it seems that the Snowbirds are much more likely to be on, or in, or near the ground, unless they find holes in old trees as woodpeckers do. In little mounds of sod thrown up by the frost a neat little entrance has often been found to lead to the snug, cosy bedroom of a Snowbird. Little hollowed places, such as field mice make in summer, have been taken and, with a little grass pulled over, have sheltered

Juncos as nicely as could be wished. A brush pile left by wood-choppers has given protection to some little mixed colony. Tall grass will do for Meadow-larks and Red-winged Blackbirds, and thorn bushes, into which the owl or bigger creatures could not crawl, may protect a spot where a covering of leaves makes comfort enough for the brave little sojourners. If we stop to think, we shall see that a tall tree top would be a much colder place ; and while the birds will make the best of what they have, they will seek far to find comfort.

THE BIRD.

HITHER thou com'st. The busy wind all night
Blew through thy lodging, where thy own warm wing
Thy pillow was. Many a sullen storm,
For which coarse man seems much the fitter born,
    Rain'd on thy bed
    And harmless head ;
And now as fresh and cheerful as the light
Thy little heart in early hymns doth sing
Unto the Providence, whose unseen arm
Curb'd them. and cloth'd thee well and warm.
All things that be praise Him : and had
Their lesson taught them when first made.

HENRY VAUGHAN.

THE EAGLE.

IT is hard to tell just how the Bald Eagle came to be our national emblem. It certainly is not from the character of the bird, for he is a sort of tramp, and sometimes even a thief. I think it must have been from his splendid power of flight, and the fine appearance he makes when he is soaring high in the sky. An eagle with his great wings outspread looks so majestic and so powerful that he might easily, in such an attitude, represent the power and greatness of a nation.

Watch a Bald Eagle getting his dinner, and much of your respect for him will vanish. If he does not steal it, he picks it up here and there like a street-dog, — a dead fish by the shore of a lake, or a dead lamb which the dogs have killed. He often watches an Osprey or Fishhawk till he sees him catch a fish, and then chases him till the hawk with a scream of disappointment drops the meal for which he has worked. The eagle picks it up, and enjoys the ill-gotten food.

Let us try to gain for our national emblem such a reputation that people will think only of the power and majesty of the eagle, and forget his lazy and thievish habits.

THE CHICKADEE.

A POET was once walking in the Concord woods in winter. The snow was deep; it was bitterly cold; his home was a long way off. He stumbled along, feeling so discouraged and so helpless that it seemed as though he must give up the struggle.

Just then he heard a bright, cheerful note, and in the twigs above him he saw a Chickadee hopping about as gaily as if it were spring, and calling such a brisk greeting that it seemed he must be really glad to see a fellow-traveler.

FIG. 2:. — Chickadee.

The poet felt ashamed that such a "little scrap of valor" could face the storm all day and all night, without ever losing his courage or even his cheerfulness; he determined to take the bird for his model, and like him be merry and brave, no matter how discouraging life might sometimes seem.

A BIRD-PARADISE.

MANY of the islands in the Pacific Ocean are so small that no people live on them; but they are large enough for multitudes of birds to make them their homes. Winter never comes to these islands, and the birds spend their whole lives on the same spot where they and their forefathers were born.

Occasionally it happens that vessels touch at these islands, that their crew may get fresh water or explore the shores and draw maps such as you have in your geographies. When these sailors or map-makers land, they find to their surprise that the birds have no fear of their strange visitors.

Instead of flying to the tops of trees or hiding in bushes, the birds walk about men's feet or light on their shoulders. When some men rode on horses, the birds lighted on the backs of the horses and picked at the saddles to see what these new contrivances were. When one explorer was picking up shells along the beach, a little bird followed him, almost snatching the shells out of his hands in its curiosity to know what the man was doing.

Why were the birds so fearless? They were no more stupid than their cousins here. Their courage came from their ignorance of the harm men could do. No men had ever hunted them. The guns which they saw and the noise of the firing meant nothing to them; to our birds it means broken wings and blood-stained feathers.

It seems a pity, does it not, that it is only where man is not known that he is not feared. If we all had treated birds kindly, man would be loved best where he is best known.

———

LITTLE birds sit on the telegraph wires ·
    And chitter, and flitter, and fold their wings ;
Maybe they think that for them and their sires,
    Stretched always, on purpose, those wonderful strings,
And perhaps the Thought that the world inspires
    Did plan for the birds, among other things.

Little things light on the lines of our lives, —
    Hopes and joys and acts of to-day,
And we think that for these the Lord contrives,
    Nor catch what the hidden lightnings say;
Yet, from end to end, His meaning arrives,
    And His word runs, underneath, all the way.

MRS. A. D. T. WHITNEY.

THE SEA-GULL.

FAR from the loud sea beaches,
    Where he goes fishing and crying,
Here in the inland garden,
    Why is the sea-gull flying?

Here are no fish to dive for;
    Here is the corn and lea;
Here are the green trees rustling.
    Hie away home to the sea!

Fresh is the river water,
    And quiet among the rushes;
This is no home for the sea-gull,
    But for the rooks and thrushes.

Pity the bird that has wandered!
    Pity the sailor ashore!
Hurry him home to the ocean,
    Let him come here no more!

High on the sea-cliff ledges,
    The white gulls are trooping and crying;
Here among rooks and roses,
    Why is the sea-gull flying?

ROBERT LOUIS STEVENSON.

HERRING GULLS AND THEIR NESTING PLACES.

A GREAT TRAVELER.

A good south wind sprung up behind,
The Albatross did follow,
And every day, for food or play,
Came to the mariner's hollo!

In mist or cloud, on mast or shroud,
It perched for vespers nine ;
While all the night, through fog-smoke white,
Glimmered the white moonshine.

IF the little birds went to school instead of being taught at home, what do you suppose would be the most important study? Arithmetic? No, indeed. The very wisest of them can't count up to ten. Grammar? Not at all. They don't even know the Parts of Speech, though they have certainly heard Exclamations enough.

Would it be geography? Yes. I suppose most birds would have to have geography every day in the week. At any rate, the old birds know enough about it, and practice almost every hour what they know.

The old Grouse you read about knew every bush and clump of ferns in his swamp, and the little paths which led up to the hill, and the pine grove above the swamp. He knew its products and its climate, where the buds and berries grew, and what kind of wind and sky meant rain.

But, after all, the Grouse would not have been the best teacher of geography the birds could have found for their school.   He knew the swamp and the woods around it, but a journey to the next swamp would have seemed to him quite a long one.

In fact, you remember, he rather prided himself on being a stay-at-home, and when his friend the Oven-bird told him about the beautiful southern forests, I can fancy him listening politely, but not caring much about them.

The Ovenbird would make a better teacher, would he not?   Think, for a moment, what he sees every year of his life: the dry oak woods of the north are his home in the summer; he knows them almost as well as the Grouse does, and can find his way about from the little brook where the fat spiders live, to the dry bank where his mate has built her little oven. Then in October he spends a few days in New York State, flies across the broad Hudson, and then on to the shores of Chesapeake Bay.   A week or two later he would be taking his way over the fallen needles of the great Georgia pines, and the next week watching the alligators in a Florida swamp.

Here a few of his friends think it warm enough to spend the winter, but he flies over the warm Gulf

Stream, over the coral islands, and comes to some little island of the West Indies, where the great palms wave along the shore. Here there are spiders enough for him and for all his northern and southern friends.

He sees the beautiful white Herons and the red Flamingoes, but side by side with him in the bushes are some friends who have made the long journey from the north in his company, Maryland Yellow-throats and Summer Yellowbirds, and higher up in the trees Redstarts and Vireos.

While the Grouse is up in the pine trees where the snow is falling steadily, the Ovenbird hides in thickest bushes from the West Indian hurricanes, which lash the tall palms on the shore.

But your geography teacher tells you about lands further away, — about the white snow fields of Green-land, about the great Pacific Ocean, and the wonder-ful jungles of India, where the tigers steal through the long grass; or the forests of the Amazon on our own side of the world, where the monkeys make rope-ladders of themselves over the streams.

I do not think there is any bird that has seen all these places; the great white Owl has traveled much in the north, and could tell many an interesting story of the hare and the grouse, which try to escape his keen eyes by turning white themselves in winter.

But he never ventures into the Amazon forests or

the Indian jungle; he is dressed too warmly to enjoy the climate, for one thing, nor does he understand the kind of hunting he would have to do there. He needs wide plains where he can fly silently for miles and miles until he finds a hare crouching behind a hummock. And the Toucan of Brazil and the Horn-bill of India would find no fruit in the barren north country.

Perhaps the greatest traveler, after all, is the bird mentioned in the verses at the head of this story.

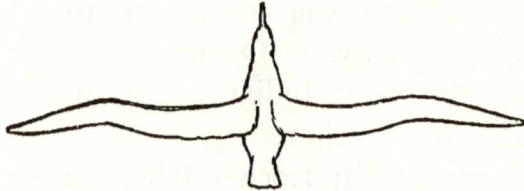

FIG. 26. — Showing Great Length of Albatross' Wings.

This traveler's name shows his manner of life, — the Wandering Albatross. He travels all over the southern seas from the Cape of Good Hope to Cape Horn and around again; people have watched him from their ships, and every one who has seen him has wondered at his huge wings and the skill with which he uses them.

He never seems to hurry or to work hard, even against a fierce wind; now on one side of the ship, now on the other, now low over the water, now high in the air, often without a stroke of his wings.

Perhaps the best testimonial he could bring, when he applied for his position as Bird School-teacher, would be the following record taken from the wing of an Albatross which the captain of a sailing vessel had caught:

"'December 8th, 1847. Ship Euphrates, Edwards, New Bedford, 16 months out. . . . Lat. 43° 00' South. Long. 148° 40' West. Thick, foggy, with rain.'

"On the opposite side it reads : ' This was taken from the neck of a Goney [Albatross], on the coast of Chili, by Hiram Luther, Dec. 20th, 1847. In Lat. 45° 50' South. Long. 78° 27' West. Taken out of a small bottle tied round the bird's neck.'

"The shortest distance between Capt. Edwards's position, about 800 miles east of New Zealand, and Capt. Luther's position off the coast of Chili in the vicinity of Juan Fernandez, is about 3400 miles. The bird, therefore, covered at least this distance in the twelve days which intervened between its release and capture."

THE REDSTART.

IN the West Indies, although there are many bright-colored birds which are natives of the islands, our little Redstart is known as Candelita, the little torch.

Unlike several of the bright-colored birds, such as the Tanager and the Indigo Bird, he does not lose his brilliant colors in the autumn; the orange patches on his shoulders gleam against his black head all winter in the tropical forests, where he flits about, spreading his yellow tail and catching insects among the leaves.

By May he is back in New England helping his mate select the best fork in a tree for their pretty nest. If you see the female searching for building material, put out wool or cotton batting, and for a reward you may see where she flies with it and find the nest.

The little Redstart is one of the unhappy birds on whom the Cowbird forces her ugly young ones, but he brings up the strangers faithfully.

Nothing but good can be said of either the male or the female Redstart; they catch countless insects, cheer us by their beauty and pretty ways, and bring up their young to be hard-working and cheerful like themselves.

THE REDSTART.

THE HUMMING BIRD.

THERE is always great excitement when a Humming Bird's nest is found. It is so rarely seen, so skilfully and beautifully made, that it seems more like a bit of bird life from fairy land than a real bird's nest. The nest is generally saddled on a dead twig and covered with the gray lichen which clothes dead twigs, so that unless you see the little mother sitting in it, you pass it by for a gray, lichen-covered knob. Look into it and see the two tiny white eggs not larger than pea beans.

If the nest looks like that of a fairy bird, the parents look even more like strangers in the Bird World. Among the great gaudy flowers of the tropics, Humming Birds probably seem more in place. Here, however, their quick whirring flight, their silence, their sudden coming and going, make the sight of one something to remember and be glad for. People who love flowers and live among them are oftenest visited by these tiny birds. Often the bird seems to have a regular route, and comes to the same garden and the same flowers at nearly the same hour of the day.

Once, while sitting on a piazza in the country, along which there grew many flowers which the Humming Bird loved, a lady saw two of them go through a very remarkable and beautiful movement. The two birds hovered in the air about ten feet apart, their wings beating so fast that it was impossible to see them. Suddenly the birds shot down and passed each other, then up, till each stopped in the position which the other one had held. This movement they repeated several times. It seemed as if the birds were executing some beautiful dance.

South and North America are the only countries which possess Humming Birds. In the eastern part of the United States we have only one species, but in California several are found, and as one goes southward, they become more numerous; in South America there are several hundred species. Among these are some of the most gorgeous colors in nature. The throat and neck feathers particularly shine with changeable colors, like brilliant jewels. The bills of the birds, too, are extremely interesting. Some are long and curved, so that the bird can feed from the honey at the bottom of the long tube-like flowers. It is a sad sight in South America to see the boxes of Humming Birds' skins pulled from their poor, bleeding little bodies and sent to the milliner's to decorate women's hats.

Our Humming Bird, the Ruby-throated, lives, as you know, on the sweet nectar of flowers. Birds often fly into the open windows in summer, and, if caught, are easily tamed. They will live on sugar and water, and many stories are told of their pretty ways in captivity. The prettiest sight, however, must have been to see them dart off happily again when their captors released them.

We have been taught how many plants need insects to bring their pollen for some other plant to fertilize their blossoms. The Humming Bird renders this service. We are not sure he would do so simply for the sweets the deep chalices contain, but he knows that where honey is insects are sure to be, and he inserts his long curved bill.

I like sometimes, on a cool, clear night in September, to think of the little Humming Birds away up in the darkness, their wings buzzing and their long bills pointing straight for the West Indies. Twice a year the little mites take a journey of thousands of miles in the night times, coming back when our spring returns and our flowers are again in bloom.

All of us know the habit of the Humming Bird of poising himself in the air and keeping up a quick vibration of his wings, so that they can hardly be seen as wings at all.

Humming Birds are said to be little centers of passion. If they do not find in a flower the honey or insects they expected, they will sometimes tear it to pieces, as if in a great rage.

The Humming Bird nest is the most exquisite little fabric you can imagine. It is like a fairy thing. Its tiny white eggs are not larger than the smallest bean, and the naked little ones when they hatch have been compared to bluebottle flies.

FIG. 27. — Rose-breasted Grosbeak.

AS FREE AS A BIRD.

EVERY good thing in the world must be earned. A bird would have less care and fewer moments of anxiety if it lived in a cage, if it were sheltered in stormy times, protected from enemies, and provided with food. But the bird prefers, as you would, I hope, to run the dangers of a free life for the sake of its pleasures.

In ordinary seasons, and for the greater part of the year, these pleasures are many. Chief among them in the case of many birds must be the joy of having wings. When an Ovenbird mounts high in air, and then, closing his wings, shoots down a hundred feet or more, it seems as if he must enjoy the rush of the air and the speed of his flight.

Hawks often soar in great curves, hardly moving their wings, but rising on the up-current of air, till they seem mere specks in the blue sky. They do this with no apparent purpose, but as if it were a sport. Some of the water birds — the Gannets, for instance — have such powerful wings that the fiercest winds cannot drive them out of their course; they circle about in tremendous storms as if they enjoyed the wild scene.

It is in nesting time, of course, that birds suffer the most anxiety. When any strange creature approaches the nest, the mother's restless eye watches anxiously. The father is often near at hand, and if the nest or young are threatened, an outcry is raised at once.

The day the young first fly and the succeeding ones, till they are skilful and strong, are times of watchfulness. But there are many happy hours even in nesting time. Bright, sunny days come, when the male sings for hours from some tree near by, and the female broods on the nest, happy to feel the warm eggs under her.

When the young are old enough to care for themselves, then the birds' holiday begins, and it often lasts till the following spring. Nothing to do now but to get food from the thick patches of weeds or the numerous insects. An eye must be kept out for the shadow of a hawk's wing, and by the game birds for the approach of a gunner; but many birds run little risk even from these enemies. Many of the birds flock together at this season; many sleep in great companies, and at night, when they go to bed, they make as much noise and have as jolly a time as a band of children.

A bird's memory is too short to remember suffering for long, and his little brain does not look forward, as ours do, to evil that may come. His nature teaches

A PAIR OF ORIOLES

him to be wide-awake, but he does not borrow trouble. When it rains, he hides in some thick shelter; when it is cold, he fluffs out his feathers; when the sun comes out, he sings again from joy. A poet once envied the fishes their "sweet, silver life wrapped in round waves," but a bird has all the pleasures that a fish can enjoy, and the sun, the warmth, and song besides.

FIG. 28. — Cedar Bird.

TO THE GREAT AND GENERAL COURT OF
MASSACHUSETTS.

*We, the Song birds of Massachusetts and their Play-
fellows, make this our humble petition.*[1]

*WE know more about you than you think we do. We
know how good you are. We have hopped about the
roofs and looked in at the windows of the houses you have
built for poor and sick and hungry people and little lame and
deaf and blind children. We have built our nests in the
trees and sung many a song as we flew about the gardens and
parks you have made so beautiful for your own children,
especially your poor children, to play in.*

*Every year we fly a great way over the country, keeping all
the time where the sun is bright and warm; and we know
that whenever you do anything, other people all over the great
land between the seas and the great lakes find it out, and
pretty soon will try to do the same thing. We know; we
know. We are Americans just as you are. Some of us, like
some of you, came from across the great sea, but most of the
birds like us have lived here a long while; and birds like us
welcomed your fathers when they came here many years ago.
Our fathers and mothers have always done their best to please
your fathers and mothers.*

[1] This petition, reduced in size from the original manuscript now
lying in the Massachusetts State House, was written by Hon. George F.
Hoar and illuminated by Miss Ellen Hale.

FIG. 29.— Song Birds of Massachusetts.

Now we have a sad story to tell you. Thought-less or bad people are trying to destroy us. They kill us because our feathers are beautiful. Even pretty and sweet girls, who we should think would be our best friends, kill our brothers and children

so that they may wear their plumage on their hats. Sometimes people kill us from mere wantonness. Cruel boys destroy our nests and steal our eggs and our young ones. People with guns and snares lie in wait to kill us, as if the place for a bird were not in the sky, alive, but in a shop window, or under a glass case. If this goes on much longer, all your song birds will be gone. Already, we are told, in some other countries that used to be full of birds, they are almost gone. Even the nightingales are being all killed in Italy.

Now we humbly pray that you will stop all this, and will save us from this sad fate. You have already made a law that no one shall kill a harmless song bird or destroy our nests or our eggs. Will you please to make another that no one shall wear our feathers, so that no one will kill us to get them? We want them all ourselves. Your pretty girls are pretty enough without them. We are told that it is as easy for you to do it as for Blackbird to whistle.

If you will, we know how to pay you a hundred times over. We will teach your children to keep themselves clean and neat. We will show them how to live together in peace and love and to agree as we do in our nests. We will build pretty houses which you will like to see. We will play about your gardens and flower beds, — ourselves like flowers on wings, — without any cost to you. We will destroy the wicked insects and worms that spoil your cherries and currants and plums and apples and roses. We will give you our best songs and make the spring more beautiful and the summer sweeter to you. Every June morning when you go out into the field, Oriole and Blackbird and Bobolink will fly after you and make the day more delightful to you; and when you go home tired at sundown, Vesper Sparrow will tell you how grateful we are. When we sit on your porch after dark, Fife Bird and Hermit Thrush and Wood Thrush will sing to you; and even Whip-poor-will will cheer up a little. We know where we are safe. In a little while all the birds will come to live in Massachusetts again, and everybody who loves music will like to make a summer home with you.

BIRDS' ENEMIES.

NONE of us know what it is to live in the midst of enemies; to go to bed at night wondering whether Indians are not hiding in the darkness waiting to burn our house and carry us off prisoners.

Many children, two hundred years ago, when the French and Indians were at war with the settlers, saw their fathers load their guns at night and go to sleep, ready to run with them to the blockhouse if the alarm were sounded.

The birds, like the early settlers, are never free from fear. Their enemies are so numerous, so fierce, so quick, that they must be constantly on the watch, and, like the early settlers, have to guard, not themselves only, but their young ones and their eggs.

Most of the birds' enemies are looking for a meal, and hope to pick the flesh off the bones of some plump Robin or Quail. A few are afraid of the sharp bills of the old birds, and so prowl about, hoping to seize the helpless young when their parents are away for a moment, or to break and open the eggs and eat the uncooked omelet which they find in them.

Some go about boldly by day, either soaring high overhead or sitting motionless on some lookout post,

and the eyes of such enemies are so sharp that most
birds prefer to keep near bushes or trees so that
they may dive into them at the first sight of their foe.
Chickadees fly from tree to tree, and if they come to
an open space they slip over, one by one, as hurriedly
as possible. A hat thrown up when they are starting
frightens them so that they hurry back to shelter.
These midday enemies are mostly hawks, swift, strong
robbers, with crooked claws and powerful bills. Some
of them have very long wings, so that they can go
like an arrow at their victim, and when they reach
him and strike their talons into his breast, the force
of their flight often strikes him to the ground, where
the hawk's hooked bill soon makes an end of the
unfortunate bird.

Other enemies fly softly about at dusk. You have
already read about the owls and know how the birds
hate the sight of them. There is another night wan-
derer whom many of the birds fear and despise as
much as they do an owl. It is an animal of which
you are probably very fond, your own gentle Pussy.
But if Pussy were four or perhaps ten times as big as
you are, and you saw her big yellow eyes glaring at
your little brothers and sisters or friends, ready to
spring at them and eat them, you would set up a cry
of warning, too, just as the wrens do when they see
her. Many a poor mother-Robin has seen her young

ones carried off by cats when they were too young to fly far, but too eager to see the world to stay any longer in the nest.

Another little animal whom you like very much is no friend of the birds. The little Red Squirrel, who runs up the tree so nimbly, scolding, and shaking his tail, and stopping to nibble a nut, eats something besides nuts if he gets a chance. I once saw two Robins who were very much excited. They scolded and flew wildly about, dashing now and then to their nest, which I could see on the limb of a tree. Presently, as I watched the nest, I saw a squirrel lift his head up only to duck it again, as the angry birds made a dash at him. The rascal was evidently squatting in the midst of the eggs, breaking them open and feasting upon the contents. It must have been a sad sight for the mother when he left the nest, those eggshells, stained and broken, which she had left so glossy and blue a few minutes before.

Another egg thief is a bird whose love for his own eggs ought to teach him better, if they get as far as love for one another in Bird World. In one of Mr. Audubon's famous pictures he has drawn a saucy Blue Jay, who has stuck his bill into an egg and holds it up ready to fly off with it. This trick he has learned with acorns and chestnuts.

The enemy that the birds would fear most would

be the snake. If you have been well brought up and
know your *Alice in Wonderland,* you remember how
frightened the pigeon was when Alice grew so tall
that her long neck reached up through the trees.
" You 're a snake," said the pigeon, and would have
nothing to do with her.

Many a poor bird, sitting in her nest, concealed
from all enemies, has heard a rustling in the leaves
and seen the flat head of the snake, the cold, shiny
eyes, and the forked tongue. If she has young in the
nest she tries to drive the snake off, and her cries
bring other birds; but sometimes the snake is too
strong for them and the young are swallowed before
the mother's eyes. Not even birds that build in ponds
are safe, for snakes can swim as well as climb. How
is it, then, that birds manage to protect themselves
from so many enemies? The list is long already, and
yet we have not mentioned the foxes, the crows, the
Butcher Bird, and other marauders and thieves.

To begin with, if the bird's enemies are sly, the
bird itself is wide-awake. Watch a wren in a stone
wall, or a Song Sparrow in a brush heap, and see how
he slips in and out like a mouse. No matter how
busily the bird is feeding or frolicking, he never forgets that danger may be near, and on the first sign of
an enemy all is silence and the place is apparently
deserted.

It is very strange to walk where birds are singing all about, and to notice that they have suddenly become silent and motionless. If you look up, there is probably a hawk flying overhead. The birds have seen him before you have, and dare not move a feather that will attract attention. Most of their long journeys are performed at night. Many of them make even their shorter journeys from place to place about their homes by slipping from bush to bush or along stone walls and thickets.

Only birds that are strong and swift of wing feel free to fly straight through the air. Some birds are so skilful in the air that they take no pains to conceal themselves; if the hawk is swift, they are swifter. It would be waste of time for most hawks to chase a swallow; the swallows know it and fly boldly about in the open sky.

To protect the young and the eggs is a harder matter. If an enemy finds these, there is no escape. The bird, therefore, tries to hide the nest or to place it out of reach. It is only when winter comes and the trees and branches are bare that we see all about us the nests which, though full last spring of eggs and young, were never noticed.

By putting the nest behind protecting leaves, under a tuft of grass or a loose piece of bark, by building it of material colored like the ground or twigs on which it rests, the bird hopes to conceal it from all strange eyes. When she sits, her own sober colors and quiet position prevent her from being noticed.

The Oriole hangs her pendent nest at the ends of long twigs, for the squirrels do not care to trust their weight at the tips of long branches, and the nest is too deep for other creatures to get into. The woodpecker's holes are too narrow to admit any enemies besides snakes, so that neither woodpeckers nor Orioles take great pains to conceal their nests.

Many birds that live on the ground have still another way of keeping enemies from discovering their nests, — a way which it takes courage to carry out, and which wins our respect. The mother bird often attracts attention to herself, and so leads us away from the nest, by pretending lameness and fluttering slowly off in the opposite direction.

Many birds, too, though very cowardly when they themselves are attacked, show surprising courage in defending their nests and young. The hen, for example, is by no means brave, but she covers her chickens with her wings at sight of a hawk and looks him boldly in the face.

When we see the birds thus kept in constant fear by such a variety of enemies, liable to attack in any place, by day or night, does it not seem hard that those to whom they can give the greatest pleasure, who ought to be their chief protectors and friends, are often their worst enemies?

Men can do them more harm than all their other enemies combined. They hunt the old birds for food, and sometimes for mere amusement; and thoughtless boys take their eggs to gratify a passing whim. Women wear the feathers and even the bodies of birds on their hats. If every one could come into Bird World as we have done, and could learn to know and love the birds, I think the Feathered Folk would have one less enemy, and by and by be much more happy and confiding.

FIG. 30. — The Bluebird.

FAMILIES IN BIRD WORLD.

THERE are often families of people, the children of which resemble one or both parents so closely that any one knowing the parents is able to recognize the children. This resemblance of parent and child is due to the law of inheritance. Children will be like their parents all through nature.

There is, however, another law not so easy to understand as the law of inheritance, according to which two children of the same parents will differ from each other in a thousand little ways. We can see this very easily among our friends; brothers and sisters are alike and yet different. Only in very rare cases is it hard to tell them apart. This law also holds true throughout nature, and though it is often hard for our eyes to see differences among animals, it is easy to see in a litter of pups or a family of kittens how different in size, marking, and disposition the different individuals are.

These two laws have been at work in the world for ages, and between them, and with the help of one or two other laws, the earth has been peopled with a wonderful multitude of plants and animals of all kinds.

Students of natural history, by looking for resem-

blances and differences, try to trace back the descent
of all these creatures and plants, and to discover how
many are descended from the same ancestor.

When books on natural history speak of this or
that family of birds, the words do not mean parents
and their four or five children; they mean all the
birds which resemble each other so closely that they
probably have descended from the same bird. It is
like a clan in Scotland, where in thousands of houses
you find people who belong to one great family; they
are all related, and many can trace their relationship
to the head or chief of their clan.

In some cases it is easy in Bird World to see the
relationship in a great family; in others it is not evi-
dent at the first glance. The Ducks, for instance,
form a great family which any one could separate;
their webbed feet, their bills, their peculiar shape, all
serve to mark them as distinct from other families
and related to each other.

Parrots form another large and easily defined family.
Owls resemble each other all over the world. In the
Flycatcher family and the Sparrow family the resemblance is not so easily seen, but close examination
shows that the birds have the same style of wing,
that the wings and tail have the same relative length
or the same general shape. Colors vary more than
the shape of the bills, wings, and feet, so that in the

same family there may be very plain or very bright
birds. It is only by examining the bill that we discover that the bright-colored Rose-breasted Grosbeak,
for instance, is really a sparrow.

Families are often related to other families; the
Ducks are related to the Swans and to the Geese.
Herons and Storks are related. One of the strangest
relationships is that between the Chimney Swift and
the Humming Bird, birds so different in appearance
and in habits. For a long time the Swift was thought
to be a member of the Swallow family, but though
his habits are similar, he is not at all a near relation.

Birds seem to know very little of their family relationships. If different species have the same habits,
they flock together. It is true the different species
of the swallow family often gather in great flocks, but
other flocks are often seen, made up of warblers,
vireos, Kinglets, and Chickadees, birds belonging to
four different families.

The Duck family and the Hen family (to which the
Grouse, Turkey, and Guinea Fowl belong) have, in one
way, been the most useful family to man, for they
have supplied so many domestic birds. The hawks
and owls have probably been the most fiercely attacked
by man. The family of perching birds, which include
nearly all our singing birds, — sparrows, thrushes,
warblers, swallows, etc., — are best beloved by man.

IF you were swimming, would you spread your fingers apart or close them? When you have answered this question and thought a little about your reasons, you will understand more easily what I am going to tell you about a bird's feather. The air through which the bird makes its way must be swept aside, just as the water is swept by your closed fingers or by the blade of an oar. If the air could blow through between the wing feathers, the bird could not get ahead.

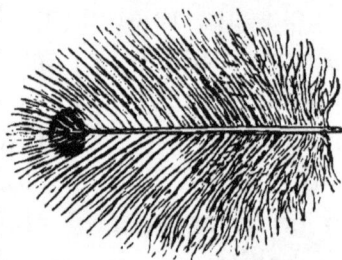

FIG. 31.—Contour Feather.

Look now at the strong feather in Fig. 32, or, better still, examine a feather itself. You see a shaft running the length of the feather, and from it runs a long row of barbs, as they are called — short, stout ones from the outer side of the shaft, longer, more slender ones from the inner side. Try to separate two of these barbs by stretching out the whole row. Do you see how they hold together? When you have finally pulled two of them apart, pass the forward one — the one nearer the tip of the feather — under the rear one, and you will see that they unite again. With a microscope you can find the hooks by which one barb holds fast to the one in front of it. Now we

FIG. 32. — Wing Feather.

understand why the air does not blow through the feathers.

The strong feathers, which the bird uses like oars, are in the wings and tail. The shorter feathers, which cover the back, breast, and head, form webs in the same way, but in their case it is to keep the bird warm and dry. When a bird has had his feathers ruffled or wet, he sits on some perch and rearranges them with his bill, so that they lie smoothly in their proper places.

Some birds have feathers which have grown in such peculiar forms that they are used in special ways. The Chimney Swift, Downy Woodpecker, and Brown Creeper have stiff or spiny tail feathers

FIG. 33.— Strong Feather of Chimney Swift.

which half support the bird in climbing. Many separate feathers of tropical birds grow into beautiful or wonderful forms. The Birds of Paradise have many such ornamental feathers.

Did you know that hair and nails were really pieces of a very peculiar skin, nothing more? They grow from the skin, and though they seem so different, they

FIG. 34. — Wing of Barn Swallow.

are really made of the same material. So with birds' feathers. They look first like little pimples in the bird's skin; out of this the feather pushes and grows till it reaches its proper size. When the feathers are worn by winds and by the twigs of trees, the new

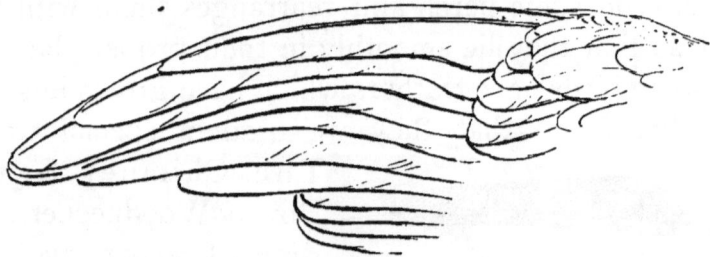

FIG. 35. — Wing of Grouse.

feather pushes up, through the skin, and the old feather falls out.

The little barbs at the tips of the smaller feathers give the color to the bird, the lower parts of the

feather being overlaid and concealed by the other
feathers. The breast feathers of a Robin, for instance,
are dull gray except at the tips, which are bright bay.

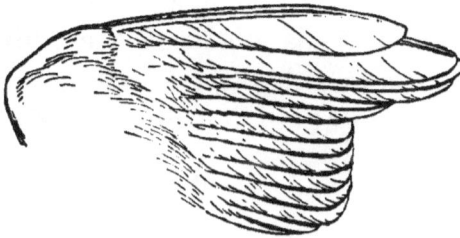

FIG. 36. — Sparrow's Wing.

Some birds wear off
the tips of these
feathers by brushing
them so constantly,
just as a broom gets
worn down, and if the
rest of the feather is
of a different color,
the bird may change his appearance greatly without
changing a feather.

You have read, or will read,
about several birds that cannot
fly. The Dodo could not, and
the Apteryx cannot to-day.
But you will never hear of a
bird without feathers. Nor
will you hear of feathered
creatures that are not birds.
Fur and scales and hair clothe
the other creatures of the
world. The mark of the bird
is to be clothed in feathers.

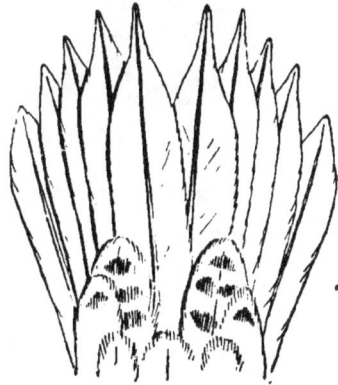

FIG. 37. — Tail of Flicker.

To fly — to go from one place in the air to
another further on — a bird must take strokes with

his wings. On the end of the wing are the long
primary feathers, like the fingers of our hand. These
and the secondaries close to them form a strong web
which the bird can hold out at full length or bend
at the elbow. The whole wing is joined to the body
at the shoulder in such a way that the wing moves
forward and down, not straight up and down. It is

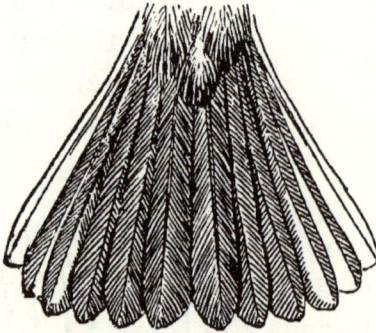

FIG. 38. — Tail of Snowbird.   FIG. 39. — Tail of Snowbird.

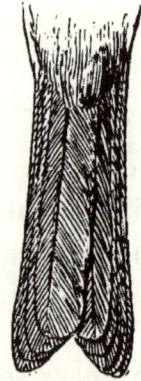

this forward motion which pushes the bird along, and
the downward stroke which keeps him from falling.
Some birds — Kingbirds, for example — take rapid
strokes, so that they fly in a straight line without
falling between the strokes. Woodpeckers, on the
other hand, fall some distance between each stroke,
so that their flight is a succession of curves.

The length of a bird's wing is important to notice.
A long, narrow wing gives a more powerful sweep

and makes a swift flyer. Notice the ease with which a swallow cuts through the air, and then compare the shape of his wing with that of the sparrow's. A long, broad wing is very useful for birds like the eagles and vultures, who spend much time soaring at great

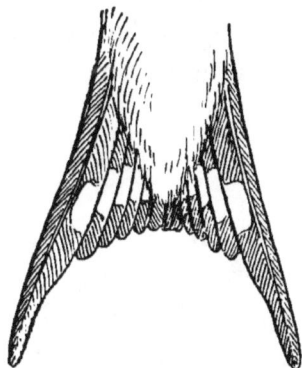

FIG. 40. — Tail of Barn Swallow.   FIG. 41. — Tail of Dove.

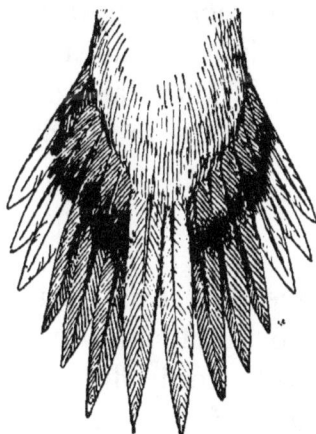

heights. The outspread wings and tail keep them up for hours with little effort on their part.

It is much harder for a bird to start to fly than to go on, unless in a strong wind. Why this is so, it would be hard for you to understand. Some birds, like the Albatross, can remain on the wing for days, but if caught and placed on the deck of a steamer, they cannot rise and fly off. On the ocean they run a long distance, flapping the water and getting under way, as it is called, before they can rise into the air.

When you read about feathers, you learned that all birds had feathers, but that there were some who could not fly. I think you have now learned enough about flight to see why this is so. The heavy birds with short wings — the Auk and the Ostrich — cannot support such weight in the air, so must get along with swimming and running and diving. The long-winged swallow and the broad-winged hawk are as much at home in the air as the fish is in the water.

FLIGHT.

Have you ever wondered why it is that a bird flies so surely and straight where he wants to go, while a butterfly flits about in such a haphazard way?

Those of you who have had to do with boats will know what ballast is, and how necessary it is to a boat's even, steady progress. The weight of the boat should be well down in the water. The bird is like a well-ballasted boat. The heavy muscles and the stomach, with its weight of food, are all in the "hold," so to speak, — all down as low as possible, — and the expanse of the wing is not great enough to out-balance this. In the case of the butterfly the wing expanse is so great and the weight of the body so little that the insect flutters about, driven out of its course by every breath of air.

A boat is so built that it floats even when no work is done with the oars, but if a bird stops flying, it will fall to the ground. The bird's flight is, therefore, more like swimming, in which a person tries not only to keep up, but to get ahead as well.

Often, however, a bird ceases to take wing strokes, but instead of falling to the earth, he glides on through the air. This is because he keeps both wings and tail spread, and the air, as you well know, will not let a broad surface fall as quickly as a narrow one. If a bird wants to fall quickly, — if a hawk, for instance, sees a mouse below him, or a lark wants to shoot down to his mate, — he shuts his tail and brings his wings close to his body. Suppose the mouse had vanished before the hawk reached the ground, the hawk, by opening tail and wings again, will stop his downward falling and turn it into an upward and onward course. The broad wings and tail help, then, to support the bird in the air, and the tail acts as a brake to check his motion.

THE SNOWY EGRET.

THIS beautiful bird takes advantage of our being in Bird World to interest us in the saving of his family from utter destruction.

The food of the Heron family is in watery places, and they get it for the most part by wading. The long legs and neck show how nature has provided the birds for their place. For their beauty she gave them an almost fatal gift. If you were to count in an audience of ladies the soft, light, graceful feathers, called aigrettes, worn in black, white, yellow, blue, — all colors, — you can guess in advance the pitiful story the bird of our lesson has to tell, for he is the Snowy Egret.

The case is one of the most pitiful in Bird World. To meet the demand of fashion, the plume-lets have to be cut from the bird when they first come to perfection. All that has been said of birds' wedding suits shows that this is the time when the wearer of the plumes is most necessary to his family. So absorbed is he in what goes to make up family life that he forgets to exercise the wary habits which the Nature-fairy sets over against her dangerous gift of beautiful adornment.

At nesting time these birds are so in love with each other and with their babies that they are stupid in watching against danger ; and this is a time when some man, who has become an expert gunner, takes

FIG. 42. — Snowy Egret.

an order for supplying a hundred or a thousand aigrettes to a millinery house. He knows where in Florida, Mississippi, or Texas marshes he may expect to find a great colony of the birds he wants. So noisy are they he has no difficulty in locating them.

You can imagine the rest of the story. It is as if

the mothers and fathers of a village were to be taken away and no provision made for four or five little children in every home.

The parents have a quick death, falling under the marksman's shot, but it takes some time for the brave little ones waiting for food to cease crying and painfully wait their release.

Remember, this had to happen that the graceful aigrettes might make a pretty hat a little prettier than something else might have made it, and you will wish to become the bird's champion to save its race from so needless a destruction.

He prayeth well, who loveth well
  Both man and bird and beast.
He prayeth best, who loveth best
  All things both great and small ;
For the dear God who loveth us,
  He made and loveth all.

COLERIDGE.

THE WOOD THRUSH.

EARLY in this book you saw what would probably
be called the handsomest song bird in Bird
World, the Scarlet Tanager; but most people would
rather live near a Wood Thrush than a Tanager, in
spite of his plain brown and white suit. For this
Thrush is the finest of all our many songsters; his
notes are as rich and sweet as an organ's or those of
a stringed instrument. Early in May he reaches
New England, but when the hot days of August
come, he stops singing, and before October he leaves
for the south, where, silent and shy, he hides in the
woods till April comes again.

Mr. Samuels says: " The thrushes are the birds that
rid the soil of noxious insects that are not preyed
upon by other birds."

Warblers capture insects in the foliage of trees;
flycatchers, those that are flying about; swallows,
those which have escaped all these; woodpeckers,
those in the larval state in the wood; wrens, nuthatches, titmice, and creepers eat the eggs on and
under the bark, but the thrushes subsist on those
which destroy the vegetation on the surface of the
earth.

THE BROWN THRUSH.

THIS is the "merry brown thrush" of the poem, whose message to children was that the world

FIG. 43. — Brown Thrasher.

would n't continue to "run over with joy" unless they were as good as could be.

Its more common name, Brown Thrasher, comes from its wren-like habit of thrashing its tail.

While it looks like the Thrushes, it acts like the wrens, and it is contended that it is not really a Thrush at all.

Very good and pleasant things are said of its dashing, exultant song. It is more distinct than most bird songs, and there are many different ways of rendering it into our kind of language. Thoreau tells us that the farmers who hear it first in planting time agree in making it say, " Drop it, drop it, cover it up, cover it up, pull it up, pull it up." The ringing notes can be heard quite a third of a mile away.

This picture only shows its general appearance. If you compare it with the Robin, you will see that the wings are shorter, and the tail longer in proportion.

In color it has rust red, but it is on the back, rather than the breast, which latter is white, with black spots shaped like arrowheads, all pointed forward. The two white bands across the wings also help to distinguish it.

It builds its nest either on the ground or in some high bush, and its eggs are speckled with reddish brown; but when it intends to sing, it is apt to fly to the topmost twig of a high tree, like another bird we have met in our Bird-World journey.

HAWKS.

I WAS once watching a flock of sparrows feeding and singing, flying after each other or up to the fence posts, when suddenly the singing stopped, and

FIG. 44. — Cooper's Hawk.

not a bird stirred a feather. I looked up, and in the sky I saw a small hawk soaring and flapping; till he was out of sight, you would have believed the field was empty; then the singing and fluttering began again. Often the little hawk comes up so silently that he sees the birds before they have a chance to "play 'possum." Then a chase begins, the little birds trying to reach bushes where they can slip into a tangle, the hawk trying to strike or seize them with his curved toes, — talons they are called.

Stories are told of small birds taking refuge with men, and of hawks so bold that they have pursued their prey into a barn or even an open window.

Fig. 45. — Head of Hawk.

The fate which awaits a bird whom the hawk overtakes is terrible enough to explain the silent fright which a hawk's appearance produces. In a

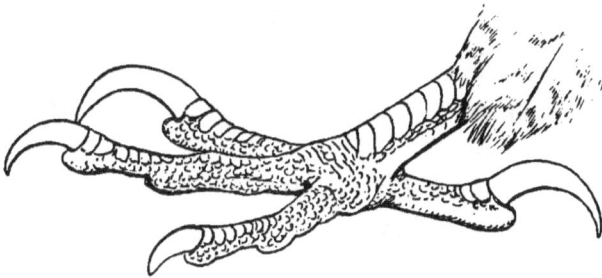

Fig. 46. — Foot of Hawk.

crowded city street I saw a hawk catch a sparrow and carry him screaming with pain and terror to the limb of an elm. The poor little fellow was dead, the sharp claws having pierced his breast. The hawk now bent over, holding the sparrow to the limb, and tore the feathers out, plucking them as we pluck a chicken.   Then he took mouthfuls of the flesh with his sharp, curved bill.

An owl would have swallowed the sparrow, feathers, bones, and all, and afterwards thrown out a ball of feathers and bones.   So that when you find the feathers of a bird in the woods, you can lay the blame on the Hawk, Cat, or Fox, but not on the Owl.

To seize a bird which can also fly needs swiftness and boldness; so that the hawks which live on other birds have long wings and a daring spirit.   Some of the fiercest are very small, while some of the large hawks rarely catch birds, but live on caterpillars, moths, frogs, and mice.

When a farmer misses his chickens one after another and, getting angry, finally takes down his gun, he may shoot a friend instead of an enemy. The bird shown in Fig. 44 and a cousin of his, called the Sharp-shinned Hawk, are the real offenders; and the large hawk, called the Hen Hawk, is innocent.

You know that when a man is tried in court for some wrongdoing, we are careful to give him a chance to defend himself, and we never call him guilty till we have proof.   The hawks cannot come to us to defend themselves, so that we ought to be very careful to get proof before we condemn them to

Copyright, 1897, by the Osprey Co.

A USEFUL HAWK.

death. We ought to be especially careful if, by kill-
ing the wrong hawk, we should destroy a friend who
protects our crops from mice and hurtful insects.

Hawks were much used in former times to hunt
with. They were carefully trained, as dogs are now,
and taught to fly after any large birds whom the
hunters wanted to kill, and to come back at the sound
of a whistle. " To hunt with hawk and hound " is a
phrase often found in old writers. Ladies often had
their favorite hawks, and carried them on their wrists.
That such a savage bird could be tamed is surprising,
but falconry seems a cruel sport which I am glad
is no longer fashionable.

BIRDS have not as much to say to each other as men have. A bird's voice is used rather more as we use a bell, to give important warnings and announcements. The fire bell warns people of danger to property. The doorbell rings when some one wishes to see a friend. The dinner-bell calls us to our food.

The parts of our speech that are most like the birds' ordinary language are what we call exclamations, — Look out! Hallo! Stop! Ho! As soon as you begin to make sentences, you are telling each other thoughts which are too difficult for birds to understand.

The common sounds which birds make can therefore be divided into two or three classes. They are generally called call notes, alarm notes, and recognition notes. The cock gives a call note when he has found something to eat; when the hens hear it, they run to the spot. Alarm notes are given by the hen when she wishes her chickens to hide under her wing, or by any bird when he is suddenly startled.

Recognition notes are used very largely by birds who travel in companies, and are given and answered constantly, so that the different members of the band may keep together. The Bobolink has a call note unlike that of any other American bird, a rich *chink*, which is often heard from the sky in the clear autumn nights. Who knows what the Bobolink is doing up there in the darkness instead of sleeping in the long grass?

The call notes are often used by the birds on various other occasions; the bird has so few words that he must make them do for several purposes. If a bird is excited, even if he is not actually afraid, he often gives his alarm note, and if he is pleased he gives his call note, without meaning to call his friends. A hen has a peculiar drawling note which she uses when she feels happy, and, by changing it a little, she expresses the unhappiness she feels in wet or unpleasant weather. A mother bird has often many little low and gentle notes which she uses to her young in the nest, and often this same baby talk is used by the parents to each other. Lastly, the young have notes of their own which generally mean, "Come! come! I am so hungry."

If birds had no other notes than these which I have mentioned, many which are now famous the world over, and beloved by nearly all people, would be almost unknown.

There is a bird in Europe whose call note is very

unpleasant and his plumage very plain; he is shy and has no amusing or pleasing ways, and yet poets in all countries have sung about him, and people have traveled long distances to hear him sing.

The song of the Nightingale or of any of the great song birds is the greatest blessing which birds have for men. If there were no singing birds, the woods and fields in spring would seem silent and dreary. The song delights men, not only because it is a cheerful or beautiful sound, but because the bird is saying something when he sings which men say too, — the best thing that they ever say.

The Nightingale, when singing, is trying to express the great love he feels for his mate, and for the little children which he has or hopes to have. First he calls her to him with a song. He sings loudly so that she can hear him wherever she is, and can come to him. Then, when they have chosen the place for their nest, and she is sitting patiently, day after day, on the eggs she has laid, he sings to her to encourage her to sit still, so that the eggs which are so precious to both of them may hatch, and the little birds, more precious even than the eggs, may be born.

If the nest is destroyed, there is nothing left to sing for, unless the birds should have courage enough to build another nest, and then the song begins again.

THE WOOD THRUSH.

SOME STRANGE BIRD MUSIC.

THE music which the Chinese make, or the noise which they call music, is not very pleasant to our ears, and the savage races make still more hideous sounds to express their joy. Birds, too, differ very much in the character of the sounds by which they express their feelings. When the Skylark knows that his mate is sitting in her nest in the wheat, and brooding the eggs from which his dear young are to hatch, he cannot keep on the ground, but mounts far into the sky, singing and singing, sometimes for ten minutes at a time. People listen and wonder at the beauty of his song.

There is a large bird, long-legged and an awkward flyer, with a long, sharp bill with which he spears unfortunate frogs. He lives in the marshes, and his brown dress is striped so that when he stands motionless among the tall grass or cat-tails, you would take him for a stake, or a bunch of the reeds themselves. He is called the Bittern, or, by the country people, Stake-Driver or Thunder-Pumper.

The last name describes very well the sound which he makes when his mate is sitting on her damp nest in the cat-tails. To cheer her and remind her that he is near and will protect her, he makes sounds which resemble the syllables *unk-a-chúnk*, made way down in one's throat, and these sounds he utters so loud that they can be easily heard half a mile away.

It seems to be a considerable undertaking for the Bittern to say all this. He first seems to fill his breast with air, and then to force it out with violent convulsions.

The notes sound as if they came through water, and in the old days, before people learned to watch closely, it was commonly believed that the Bittern put his bill into a hollow reed, or that he stuck his bill into the mud and water.

The woodpeckers express their feelings in a very characteristic way. The bill which we have seen them use for a chisel now becomes a drumstick, and beats on some dry limb a tattoo which can be heard far through the forest. The Flicker, who, you remember, has become more civilized than many of his family, has a fancy for a finer kind of a drum; he sometimes beats a tin roof or tin pan, often returning to the same spot day after day.

All these strange sounds made by the woodpeckers and the Bittern express to their mates the same feelings which the Skylark puts into beautiful song.

BIRD BILLS.

ON the two following pages are the heads of several different birds, — birds not only of different kinds, but of different families and of very different ways of life. Some of them belong to families about which you have already read. You can find a back-woodsman among them with his chisel, and a Grouse with his all-round bill, useful for crushing grain, gathering fruit, or seizing insects. The Flamingo and Duck both strain water through their bills, but the Flamingo turns his upside down so that you could almost say that he stood on his head to eat. Some of the other birds have bills of very strange shape. The gypsy Crossbill has a pair of scissors with which he cuts pine seeds, and the Humming Bird has a tube that enters the deepest flowers. Look through your book for birds of other families, Herons, Owls, Hawks, and Gulls; compare their bills with these, and with each other, and try to find out how each bird is helped by the particular shape of his bill.

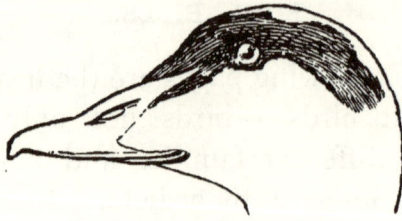

Eider Duck.

Grouse.

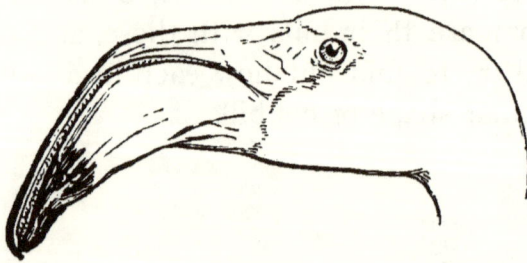

Flamingo.

FIG. 47. — Bird Bills:

196

Nuthatch.

Humming Bird.

Chimney Swift.

Hairy Woodpecker.

Red-winged Blackbird.

Crossbill.

Cardinal.

FIG. 48. — Bird Bills.

APPENDIX.

———◆◦◆———

YOU will find on following pages some keys, as they are called, which are to help you unlock some of the secrets of Bird World, and particularly to help you learn the names of any strange birds which you may meet. Be sure to remember that you may often, even with their help, make mistakes, and keep a sharp watch of any bird which you think you have identified, to see whether its actions, voice, or habits may strengthen or weaken your confidence that you are right.

Your eyes need be very sharp to work with the keys. They will ask you whether the bird had a rounded tail or a square one, whether the bill was long or short or stout or slender, what the colors were and where they were.

Perhaps it will help you to observe a living bird accurately, if you study as closely as you can the bird pictures on the pages of the book. Their colors, it is true, are not given except in a few cases, but you can see that the tail feathers of some have " thumbmarks" of some light color, that there are bars across the wings of others, and that these bars are formed sometimes of solid color, sometimes by rows of spots. Examine the tails to see whether the outer or inner feathers are the longer ; you will see that some tail feathers are sharp and probably stout. The bills will show many points of difference, and tell much about the birds' feeding habits.

[NOTE. The following key includes about fifty of the commonest summer residents of northeastern United States. The Owls, Hawks, Swallows, and one or two other birds whose general appearance serves to identify them, have been omitted in order to simplify the key as much as possible. It is not expected that young children will be able to use the key without assistance, and it is hoped that in any case it will serve merely as an incentive to further and closer observation of the living bird.]

BIRDS GROUPED BY A COLOR STANDARD.

BIRDS SHOWING MUCH BROWN.

A. Upper parts plain brown ; under parts white, or white with streaks or spots.

B. Upper parts streaked ; under parts light, or lighter colored.

C. Fawn-colored.

D. Brownish-olive.

> *A.* (1) Not streaked or spotted below.
>> *a.* Longer than a Robin.   Cuckoo.
>> *b.* Small bird with short tail.   House Wren.
>
> *A.* (2) Spotted or marked below.
>> *a.* Tail very long.   Brown Thrasher.
>> *b.* Head browner than back and tail; entire under parts heavily marked.   Wood Thrush.
>> *c.* Head, back, and tail tawny; breast lightly spotted.   Wilson's Thrush.   Veery.
>
> *B.* (1) Bird larger than a Robin.
>> *a.* Tail feathers white ; breast yellow with a black crescent.   Lives in grassy fields.   Meadow Lark.
>> *b.* Rump white; flight undulating.   Generally lights on the side of a large limb or tree trunk.   Flicker.
>> *c.* Rarely seen before dusk.   Whip-poor-will.

B. (2) Small birds with the sparrow bill.
> Breast streaked.
>> *a.* Flight nervous, jerky. Common everywhere. Song bright and cheerful. Song Sparrow.
>> *b.* Tail shorter than in *a*; a line over each eye and through the crown. Lives in grassy fields. Song weak. Savanna Sparrow. (See also Gray Birds.)
>
> Breast not streaked.
>> *a.* Tail long, notched ; breast ashy gray. Crown chestnut; black line through eye. Common about dooryards ; not at all shy. Chipping Sparrow.
>> *b.* Throat whitish ; breast grayish ; crown and wings chestnut in spring. Lives in swampy places ; rather shy. Swamp Sparrow.
>> *c.* Bill light-colored ; breast buffy-white. Lives in bushy pastures. Field Sparrow.
>> *d.* Bill stout ; throat (in male) black ; wing bars white ; sides of head chestnut. (Female brown above, dirty white below.) Common in city and village streets. English Sparrow.

C. Fawn-colored. Black line through the eye ; tail tipped with yellow. Often shows a crest. Cedar Bird.

D. Brownish-olive. Under parts white, streaked with black. Walks. Common in woodland. Ovenbird.

BIRDS MOSTLY GRAY.

A. Olive-gray.   Rarely, if ever, seen on the ground.
B. Brownish-gray.   Back streaked.
C. Slate-gray.

A. (1)   Birds that sit on exposed perches ; tail held directly beneath the bird.

    a.   No conspicuous wing-bars.   Bird jerks the tail after alighting.   Note, *phœ-be*.   Phœbe.

    b.   Two white wing-bars; tail not jerked.   Note, *pee-ee-wee*.   Wood Peewee.

    c.   Resembles *b*, but smaller.   Note, a sharp *che-bec*, snapped out with a jerk of the head.   Chebec, or Least Flycatcher.

A. (2)   Birds that hunt in the branches of trees.   Tail quite short.

    a.   White line over eye.   Song made up of broken phrases.   Red-eyed Vireo.

    b.   No white line.   Song a slow, continuous warble.   Warbling Vireo.   (Cf. p. 199 *B* (2), *a*.)

B.   A sparrow, seen on the ground or at the edges of fields.

    a.   Breast streaked ; tail shows two white outer feathers.   Song strong and sweet.   Vesper sparrow.

C.   *a*.   Found in bushy places about houses.   Cap and tail black.   Catbird.

BLACK AND WHITE BIRDS.

A. Upper parts black, streaked or spotted with white.

    a. Larger than an English Sparrow. Bill stout; back white; wings spotted with white. Male has a red patch on the back of head. Found in winter also. Downy Woodpecker.

    b. Smaller than an English Sparrow. Bill slender; entire bird striped with black and white. Black and White Creeper.

B. Whole head, crown, cheeks, and throat black. Large birds.

    a. Rose color on the breast. Wings and back showing white. Rose-breasted Grosbeak.

    b. Sides of breast chestnut. Tail showing large, white spots. Common in clearings. Chewink or Towhee Bunting.

C. Head not wholly black. Breast and belly white.

    a. Larger than sparrow. Entire under parts white; tail tipped with white. Kingbird.

    b. Smaller than sparrow. Throat and cap black. Feeds among branches, to which it clings. Chickadee.

D. Whole under parts black. Lives in grassy fields. Bobolink.

BIRDS SHOWING CONSIDERABLE YELLOW OR ORANGE.

A.　Birds showing black and yellow, or black and orange.

B.　Birds showing yellow but no black.

C.　Top of head yellow.

　　A. (1)　Orange and black.　(Females without orange.)

　　　　　　a.　Larger than sparrow.　Bill long, back yellow, breast orange.　Note, a loud whistle.　Oriole.

　　　　　　b.　Smaller than sparrow.　Mostly black, showing patches of orange at the shoulders, and yellow in the outspread tail.　Redstart.

　　A. (2)　Yellow and black.　Birds all smaller than sparrow.

　　　　　　a.　Mostly light yellow.　Forehead, wings, and tail black.　Goldfinch.　(Female without black.)

　　　　　　b.　Throat yellow.　Black band through the eye. Hides in bushes near water.　(Female without black.)　Maryland Yellow-throat.

　　　　　　c.　Throat black; sides of head yellow.　Lives in evergreens.　Black-throated Green Warbler.

　　B. (1)　Entire bird yellow; wings and tail duller.　Song, bright, lively.　Summer Yellowbird.

　　B. (2)　Throat yellow.

　　　　　　a.　Common in street trees.　Song made up of loud, rich phrases.　Yellow-throated Vireo.

　　　　　　b.　Common in pines.　Song, a slow trill.　Pine Warbler.

　　C. (1)　Under parts white; a narrow strip of chestnut along the sides.　Found in clearings and roadside bushes. Chestnut-sided Warbler.

HALF THE BIRD OR MORE SOME SHADE OF RED.

(For birds showing patches of red or orange, see Black, and Black and Orange.)

A. Head rose red. Back and tail brownish. Purple Finch.

B. Entire bird scarlet, except black wings and tail. Scarlet Tanager.

C. Breast bay; head black; wings and tail brown. Robin.

BIRDS CHIEFLY BLACK.

A. Seen chiefly on the ground.

> *a.* Larger than a pigeon. Note *caw*. Crow.
>
> *b.* Larger than a robin. Bill and tail long. Head and back glossy, with purple or bronze reflections. Crow Blackbird or Purple Grackle.
>
> *c.* A little smaller than a robin. Male has scarlet epaulets. Bill long, sharp. (Female blackish-brown, streaked.) Red-winged Blackbird.
>
> *d.* Smaller than *c.* Head rich brown. Walks on the ground, often near cattle. (Female dull brown.) Cowbird.

B. Seen always in the air.

> *a.* Wings long, curved; tail short, cigar-shaped. Chimney Swift.

BLUE OR BLUE-GRAY BIRDS.

A. Larger than a Robin.

> *a.* Wings and tail marked with black and white; collar black. Seen in trees. Blue Jay.
>
> *b.* No black; collar white. Seen flying over water or near it. Kingfisher.

B. Smaller than a Robin.

> *a.* Entirely blue, except brown wings and tail. Bird the size of a sparrow; seen on the tops of trees or in thickets. (Female brown.) Indigo Bird.
>
> *b.* Breast chestnut. Larger than a sparrow. Seen in orchards or near country houses. Bluebird.
>
> *c.* Blue-gray; under parts white; tail short. Seen on the trunks or large limbs of trees, often with head downward. Nuthatch.

COMMON SUMMER BIRDS OF NEW ENGLAND.

FOUND NEAR HOUSES, IN ORCHARDS, OR ALONG STREETS.

Robin.

Cuckoo.

Chebec.

Kingbird.

Catbird.

Goldfinch.

Cedar Bird.

Wood Thrush.*

Screech Owl.

Red-eyed Vireo.*

Yellow-throated Vireo.

House Sparrow.

Song Sparrow.

Barn Swallow.

Redstart.

Crow Blackbird.

Chimney Swift.

Oriole.

Phœbe.

Flicker.

Cowbird.

Bluebird.

Purple Finch.

Chickadee.*

House Wren.

Humming Bird.

Warbling Vireo.

Yellow Warbler.

Chipping Sparrow.

Cliff Swallow.

White-bellied Swallow.

Rose-breasted Grosbeak.

Downy Woodpecker.

IN GROVES.

Sparrow Hawk.

IN OPEN WOODS.

Mourning Dove.

FOUND IN WOODS.

Crow.

Ovenbird.

Nuthatch.

Barred Owl.

Scarlet Tanager.

Sharp-shinned Hawk.

Black-throated Green Warbler.

Grouse.

Blue Jay.

Wood Pewee.

Pine Warbler.

Whip-poor-will.

Black and White Creeper.

* Found also in woods.

FOUND IN MEADOWS.

Bobolink.
Bay-winged Bunting.

Meadowlark.
Savanna Sparrow.

FOUND IN BUSHY PASTURES.

Chewink.
Brown Thrasher.
Night Hawk.
Chestnut-sided Warbler.

Quail.
Indigo Bird.
Field Sparrow.

FOUND IN SWAMPY PLACES.

Veery.
Wood Duck.
Marsh Hawk.
Red-winged Blackbird.

Bittern.
Green Heron.
Swamp Sparrow.
Maryland Yellow-throat.

FOUND ON RIVER OR LAKE SHORES.

Kingfisher.
Spotted Sandpiper.

Bank Swallow.

FOUND SOUTH AND WEST OF NEW ENGLAND.

Cardinal Grosbeak.
Carolina Wren.

Red-headed Woodpecker.
Turkey Buzzard.

COMMON WINTER BIRDS OF NEW ENGLAND.

Grouse.	Crow.
Kinglet.	Blue Jay.
Chickadee.	Nuthatch.
Screech Owl.	Butcher Bird.
Goldfinch.	Purple Finch.
Tree Sparrow.	Brown Creeper.
Red-shouldered Hawk.	Downy Woodpecker.

IN SOUTHERN NEW ENGLAND, ESPECIALLY NEAR THE SEA.

Robin.	Flicker.
Snowbird.	Song Sparrow.
Meadow Lark.	

OCCASIONAL WINTER VISITORS.

Redpoll.	Cedar Bird.
Snowflake.	Snowy Owl.
Red Crossbill.	Pine Grosbeak.

BIRDS IN WHICH THE TWO SEXES ARE ALIKE.

Gull.	Blue Jay.	Screech Owl.
Heron.	Song Sparrow.	Kingbird.
Crow.	Chipping Sparrow.	Meadow Lark.
Phœbe.	Bank Swallow.	Red-eyed Vireo.
Cuckoo.	Ovenbird.	Brown Thrasher.
Catbird.	House Wren.	Nuthatch.
Swift.	Chickadee.	Brown Creeper.
Grouse.	Cedar Bird.	Wood Thrush.
Sandpiper.		

BIRDS IN WHICH THE TWO SEXES ARE MARKEDLY UNLIKE.

Oriole.	Bobolink.	Humming Bird.
Chewink.	Bluebird.	Barn Swallow.
Cowbird.	Goldfinch.	Red-winged Blackbird.
Tanager.	Indigo Bird.	Rose-breasted Grosbeak.
Purple Finch.	Redstart.	

BIRDS IN WHICH THE TWO SEXES ARE SIMILAR, BUT DISTINGUISHABLE.

Quail.	Flicker.	Crow Blackbird.
Hawks.	Kingfisher.	Downy Woodpecker.
Yellow Warbler.		

SOME BRILLIANT MALES WHO CHANGE INTO PLAIN CLOTHES IN THE FALL.

Bobolink.	Goldfinch.	Tanager.	Indigo Bird.

BIRDS ACCUSED OF DOING HARM IN FARM OR GARDEN.

These birds are still on trial. Perhaps you can form an opinion about some of them from what you have read.

Large Hawks.	Bobolink.
Screech Owl.	Catbird.
Sapsucker.	Cedar Bird.
Kingbird.	Butcher Bird.
Jay.	Crow Blackbird.
Crow.	Red-winged Blackbird.
Robin.	English Sparrow.

BIRDS UNDOUBTEDLY INJURIOUS.

Cooper's Hawk.	Sharp-shinned Hawk.

BIRDS UNIVERSALLY CONSIDERED BENEFICIAL TO MAN.

Name of Bird.	*Enemy Destroyed.*
Phœbe.	Gnats.
Oriole.	Beetles.
Cuckoo.	Tent Caterpillars.
Kinglet.	Insects' Eggs.
Chickadee.	Insects' Eggs.
Brown Creeper.	Insects' Eggs.
Flicker.	Ants.
Bluebird.	Grubs.
Nuthatch.	Grubs.
Swallows.	Flies.
Warblers.	Caterpillars.
Red-eyed Vireo.	Caterpillars.
Meadow Lark.	Grasshoppers.
Chipping Sparrow.	Currant Worms.
Rose-breasted Grosbeak.	Potato Bugs.
Downy Woodpecker.	Borers.

INDEX.

Albatross, 145–149, 177.
Audubon, 98.

Bills, 27, 28, 41, 79, 100, 102, 195–197.
Bird Language, 190–192.
Bird Music, 193, 194.
Bittern, 193, 194.
Bluebird, 15–17, 168.
Blue Jay, 56, 57, 164.
Bobolink, 117–120.
Bob White, 95–97.
Brown Creeper, 26, 27.
Brown Thrush, 184, 185.
Burrowing Owl, 35, 80.

Cardinal, 197.
Carolina Wren, 135.
Catbird, 75–78.
Cedar Bird, 37–39, 157.
Cherry Bird, 38.
Chickadee, 26, 27, 32, 141, 163.
Chimney Swift, 93, 94, 173, 197.
Chipping Sparrow, 52, 53, 60.
Cowbird, 14, 123–125.
Crossbill, 121, 122, 197.
Crow, 101.

Diagram of bird, 17.
Dove, 177.
Downy Woodpecker, 26, 41–43, 45.
Duck's Bill, 196.
Duck's Foot, 91.

Eagle, 140.
Eggs, 59–62.
Enemies, Birds', 162–168.
English Sparrow, 24, 25, 50.

Families, 169–171.
Feathers, 103–105, 172–178.
Fish Hawk, 80, 92, 140.
Flamingo, 195, 196.
Flicker, 44–46, 93, 175.
Flight, 178, 179.
Food, 26–28, 100–102.

Golden-winged Woodpecker, 44.
Goldfinch, 1, 2.
Grebe, 128, 129.
Grouse, 21–23, 93, 145–147, 174, 196.
Gull Dick, 29, 30.
Gypsy Birds, 121, 122.

Hawks, 186–189.
Heron, 180.
House Wren, 68–72.
Humming Bird, 105, 151–154.

Indigo Bird, 19, 20.
Islands, 142, 143.
Ivory-billed Woodpecker, 46.

Junco, 137.

Kingbird, 63–66.
Kinglet, 26.

Marsh Wren, 71, 72.
Migration, 18, 98, 115, 131–134, 146.

Nest of
Bobolink, 120.
Chipping Sparrow, 52.
Eave Swallow, 80.
Goldfinch, 2.
Humming Bird, 82, 154.
Kingbird, 65.
Oriole, 81.
Osprey, 80.
Phœbe, 4.
Robin, 8.
Song Sparrow, 52.
Tailor Bird, 83.
Woodpecker, 42.
Wren, 68, 70, 72.
Yellowbird, 14.
Yellow-throated Vireo, 106.
Nests, 59–61, 79–83, 166, 167.
Night in Bird World, 54, 55.
Nuthatch, 26, 197.

Oriole, 11, 12, 81, 82.
Osprey, 79, 80, 140.
Ostrich, 92, 127, 178.
Ovenbird, 23, 146, 147, 155.
Owls, 31–35.
Burrowing, 35.
Screech, 34.
Snowy, 35.

Passports, Bird, 113–116.
Petition, Song Birds', 158–161.
Phœbe, 3–5, 98.

Quail, 95–97.

Redstart, 112, 124, 125, 150.
Red-winged Blackbird, 89, 90, 197.
Robin, 6–10, 164.
Robin "roosts," 9.
Rose-breasted Grosbeak, 154.
Ruff, 126, 127.

Sapsucker, 47, 48.
Scarlet Tanager, 36.
Screech Owl, 34.
Snowbird, 176.
Snowy Egret, 180–182.
Snowy Owl, 35.
Song Sparrow, 51, 52, 82, 92.
Sparrows, 24, 49–53, 175.
Chipping, 52, 53, 60.
English, 24, 25, 50.
Song, 51, 52.
Tree, 27, 135–137.
Summer Warbler, 13, 14.
Summer Yellowbird, 13, 14.
Swallows, 68, 84–88.
Barn, 86–88, 99, 174, 177.
Eave, 80.
White-bellied, 68.

Tailor Bird, 83.
Thistlebird, 1.
Toes, 91–94.
Tongue of
Humming Bird, 102.
Woodpecker, 43, 102.
Toucan, 28.
Tree Sparrow, 27, 135, 137.

Vireos, 124.
Red-eyed, 106.
Yellow-throated, 106–112.

Warblers, 67.
Wings, 49, 97, 103, 176, 177.
Winter, Bird World in, 135–139.
Wood Duck, 130.
Woodpeckers, 40–48, 194, 197.
   Downy, 26, 41–43, 45.
   Flicker, 44–46.
   Golden-winged, 44.
   Ivory-billed, 46.
   Red-headed, 66.

Woodpecker — *continued.*
   Yellow-bellied, 47, 48.
Wood Thrush, 183.

Yellow-bellied Woodpecker, 47.
Yellow-throated Vireo, 106–112.
Yellow-winged Woodpecker, 47, 48.
Young birds, 61.
   how fed, 46, 99.